Tried and Convicted

Tried and Convicted

*How Police, Prosecutors, and Judges
Destroy Our Constitutional Rights*

Michael D. Cicchini

ROWMAN & LITTLEFIELD PUBLISHERS, INC.
Lanham • Boulder • New York • Toronto • Plymouth, UK

Published by Rowman & Littlefield Publishers, Inc.
A wholly owned subsidiary of The Rowman & Littlefield Publishing Group, Inc.
4501 Forbes Boulevard, Suite 200, Lanham, Maryland 20706
www.rowman.com

10 Thornbury Road, Plymouth PL6 7PP, United Kingdom

British Library Cataloguing in Publication Information Available

Library of Congress Cataloging-in-Publication Data

Cicchini, Michael D., 1967-
Tried and convicted : how police, prosecutors, and judges destroy our constitutional rights / Michael
D. Cicchini.
p. cm.
Includes bibliographical references and index.
ISBN 978-1-4422-1717-1 (cloth : alk. paper) -- ISBN 978-1-4422-1719-5 (electronic)
1. Civil rights--United States. 2. Criminal justice, Administration of--Corrupt practices--United
States. 3. Judicial corruption--United States. I. Title.
KF4749.C525 2012
345.73--dc23

2012010467

The paper used in this publication meets the minimum requirements of American National
Standard for Information Sciences Permanence of Paper for Printed Library Materials,
ANSI/NISO Z39.48-1992.

Printed in the United States of America

To (the memory of) my mother Clare Cicchini,
for telling me to write a book

Special thanks to Janet Rosen of Sheree Bykofsky Associates, Inc., and to
Suzanne Staszak-Silva and Christopher Basso of
Rowman & Littlefield Publishers, Inc.

Table of Contents

Disclaimer—Read This First!

This book is *not* legal advice, nor should it be used for legal research or any purpose other than entertainment and enjoyment. Neither the author nor the publisher is responsible for any actions taken, or decisions made, by readers of this book. Reading this book, or even contacting the author of this book, does not create an attorney-client relationship. If you have any legal questions, or think you may have legal issues of any kind, immediately consult a licensed attorney in your state. No information in this book should be used as a substitute for talking to a licensed attorney who is knowledgeable about the ever-changing laws in your state.

There are at least four reasons why you should *not* rely on this book for legal advice, or for any other purpose other than entertainment and enjoyment. First, most if not all of the laws discussed in this book will vary from state to state. For example, what is legal in one state may be illegal in another. Similarly, what may be a defense to a crime in one state may not be a defense to a crime in another state. Even the U.S. Constitution will have different interpretations depending on the particular state in which it is being applied. For example, a police action that may violate a citizen's constitutional rights in one state may be perfectly legal conduct in another state. This book may only discuss the most interesting, and not necessarily the most common, laws and interpretations.

Second, many if not most of the laws in our country are heavily dependent on a "facts and circumstances" analysis. This means that the slightest change in a particular person's set of facts and circumstances could lead to a dramatically different outcome under the law. No single book can adequately address all of those subtleties, and this book is certainly not intended to do so. Only a licensed attorney in your state will be able to properly assess the subtleties of your particular legal question or issue, and give you sound legal advice based on your specific fact situation.

Third, laws are constantly changing. Federal and state legislatures are always drafting new laws and amending old ones. Even the U.S. Constitution is subject to a constantly changing landscape. For example, the constitutional rights of due process and confrontation are frequently evolving in light of new judicial interpretations. What was current at the time this book was written may not be current by the time you read it, or even by the time the book is published.

Fourth and finally, this book simply doesn't cover all of the laws that might be relevant to a particular situation; instead, it may discuss only the most interesting laws, or only the most interesting aspect of a particular constitutional right. For example, while chapter 4 discusses your right to remain silent after the police read you your *Miranda* rights, it does not address the issue of pre-*Miranda* silence, which is governed by a different body of law. Again, only a licensed attorney in your state will be able to properly advise you based on your facts and the relevant and current law in your state.

Having said all of that, please enjoy your read as you explore some of the most interesting aspects of our constitutional law.

Introduction

Our Constitution

I can't pinpoint the precise day and time, but I'm convinced that somewhere around March of 2008 the Constitution of the United States hit a low point in its rich history. The place was the state of Wisconsin. The event was the upcoming election for a seat as a justice on the state supreme court. The subtext was a recent conviction in a homicide trial in one of the state's counties.

There had been a legal dispute in the homicide case over a piece of evidence—a damning letter accusing the defendant of murder. The prosecutor in the case wanted to use the letter and the accusations within it to help him convict the defendant. The defendant wanted to exclude the letter from the prosecutor's case because the author of the letter—the person making the damning allegations—was deceased. Therefore, if the letter were to be used at trial, the defendant would not have the opportunity to cross-examine or to challenge the letter, its accusations, or its author.

It all boiled down to one huge legal issue. The case dealt with the confrontation clause of the U.S. Constitution, which gives a defendant the right to confront, or cross-examine, both the accuser and the accusation.[1] Such cross-examination is critical in exposing the motives of the accuser and testing the reliability of the accusation itself. Despite the clear purpose of the confrontation clause, however, the law was actually far from well settled, and was strenuously debated in the homicide case. The case had dragged on for years, but had not yet reached the point of a jury trial when, through a special direct appeal, the legal issue regarding the use of the letter was resolved by the Wisconsin Supreme Court.[2]

Justice Louis Butler, the justice whose seat would soon be coming up for reelection on the Wisconsin Supreme Court, took a strict view of the Constitution and wanted meaningful protection for defendants and their right of confrontation. His view was both historically accurate and true to the recent decisions of the U.S. Supreme Court, which had just (arguably) breathed new life into a previously listless confrontation clause.[3] The remaining justices, however, preferred a different approach. They wanted to create a new rule that, by their own admission, was specifically designed to *neutralize* a defendant's right to confront, or cross-examine, the accusers and the accusations.[4] Regardless of which side you came down on, however, there was no question that this case would have a huge impact on our constitutional rights.

In the end, the other justices got their way over Butler, in a 6–1 vote. Then, based on their decision, the trial judge in the homicide case had to allow the prosecutor to use the letter at trial, and the defendant was convicted.[5] The jury members interviewed after the trial said that the letter—the author of which the defendant was never able to confront or cross-examine— was the single biggest reason they returned a verdict of guilt.[6]

■ ■ ■

Butler's seat on the supreme court then came up for reelection, and there was a lot of television advertising in what turned out to be a hotly contested race. (In Wisconsin, unlike in other states, supreme court justices are elected, not appointed.) In March of 2008, a third-party advertisement was aired against Butler and in support of his opponent in the election. The television ad was released after the homicide trial in which the defendant had been convicted based largely, if not entirely, on the letter that could not be cross-examined. The ad stated: "We count on judges to use practical common sense to keep violent criminals behind bars. But faced with an unspeakable crime, Justice Louis Butler almost jeopardized the prosecution of a murderer because he saw a technicality."[7]

A sick feeling washed over me when I first saw and heard this ad. There were so many things wrong with this. First, at the time of Butler's opinion, the defendant was not a "violent criminal." Not only had he been released on bond for many years during his pending homicide case and committed no crimes whatsoever, but, more importantly, he had only been *accused* of homicide and was presumed innocent.

Second, whether there was an "unspeakable crime" was unknown to Justice Butler—and to every other justice, for that matter—at the time he wrote his opinion. But, more importantly, it was not the role of Justice Butler, or any other justice on the state's highest court, to judge the guilt or innocence of the defendant prior to his trial. Rather, Butler and the others were there to interpret the law, and not the facts, for the trial judge presiding over the homicide case.

Third, this ad was celebrating a conviction that was obtained primarily because of a letter that, according to the ad itself, the jury described as "the most important piece of evidence they saw."[8] This piece of evidence, of course, was never confronted or cross-examined by the defendant. It is difficult to have much confidence in such an outcome.

Fourth, and most significantly, the issue on which Butler ruled involved the United States Constitution and, more specifically, the right of an accused to cross-examine the accuser at trial. Neither the Constitution, nor its confrontation clause, is a "technicality." Rather, the constitution is the very foundation of our freedom, yet this ad, which supported a candidate for the state's highest court, had trivialized it beyond belief.

I knew what would happen. This ad would win votes. Our popular culture celebrates a hypervigilant, "tough on crime" mentality, even when no crime has been proved. It demands that anyone accused of a crime go straight to prison, if not worse. It also assumes than anyone who dares to present a defense to the charges against him or her must be taking advantage of some "technicality" or loophole. I knew that this ad would strike a chord with many voters. I also predicted that Justice Butler would be defeated. And I was right.[9]

■ ■ ■

In this book I will show you why the Constitution is not a mere technicality. Rather, it is the foundation for the very freedoms that many of us are still able to enjoy. Further, I will show you how our ever-expanding and often irrational criminal justice system has grown beyond anything that is necessary or even desirable for the protection of its citizens.[10] Our system commonly ensnares good and ordinary people from all walks of life, often for things that most of us would be shocked to learn are considered criminal. This makes our Constitution of vital importance for many of us. However, in order for the Constitution to protect any of us, it must protect all of us.

I will then take you on a tour of many of our individual constitutional rights—including the right of confrontation discussed in this introduction—and show you just how fragile each of them actually is. During our exploration of these individual rights, I will also show you precisely how the police, prosecutors, and judges—all of whom are an integral part of today's hypervigilant, "tough on crime" environment—go about circumventing and destroying our constitutional rights. Finally, I will discuss what can and should be done about this in order to breathe renewed life into our constitutional protections.

Thank you for joining me on this tour of the United States Constitution and our criminal justice system.

NOTES

1. "In all criminal prosecutions, the accused shall enjoy the right . . . to be confronted with the witnesses against him." United States Constitution, Sixth Amendment, at topics.law.cornell.edu/constitution/sixth_amendment (accessed March 19, 2010).

2. The facts, legal issues, and rulings in the homicide case discussed throughout this introduction can be found in *State v. Jensen*, 2007 WI 26, www.wisbar.org/res/sup/2007p/2004AP002481.pdf (accessed March 19, 2010).

3. Up to this point in time, the U.S. Supreme Court decisions that had altered the confrontation-clause landscape were *Crawford v. Washington*, 541 U.S. 36 (2004), and *Davis v. Washington*, 547 U.S. 813 (2006).

4. In *State v. Jensen*, 2007 WI 26, at ¶ 52, the court stated: "In essence, we believe that in a post-*Crawford* world the broad view of forfeiture by wrongdoing espoused by Friedman and utilized by various jurisdictions since *Crawford*'s release is essential." In other words, the court was changing the law in order to circumvent, rather than apply, the Supreme Court's decision in *Crawford v. Washington*. For a deeper analysis of this issue, see Michael D. Cicchini, "Judicial (In)Discretion: How Courts Circumvent the Confrontation Clause Under Crawford and Davis," 75 *Tennessee Law Review* 753 (2008), at cicchinilaw.com/Articles.htm (accessed March 21, 2010).

5. *State v. Jensen*, case no. 02-CF-314, Wisconsin Circuit Court Access, entries 237 and 658, at wcca.wicourts.gov/courtRecordEvents.xsl;jsessionid=A6863FEBAA1FEA7E12445F5C7C2872D4.render6?caseNo=2002CF000314&countyNo=30&cacheId=63CDC70DD4D9E15C2E60B431316F6623&recordCount=19&offset=6&linkOnlyToForm=false&sortDirection=ASC (accessed March 19, 2010).

6. Viveca Novak, "Wisconsin Judgment Day, the Sequel," March 21, 2008, at www.factcheck.org/elections-2008/wisconsin_judgment_day_the_sequel.html (accessed March 19, 2010).

7. Ibid.

8. Ibid.

9. Shortly after Justice Butler was defeated in his bid for reelection to the Wisconsin Supreme Court, the U.S. Supreme Court decided the case of *Giles v. California*. In *Giles*, the Court decided the identical issue on which Butler had dissented from his colleagues, and which probably cost him his bid for reelection. The U.S. Supreme Court vindicated Butler, holding that *his* interpretation of the constitution was the correct one. See *Giles v. California*, 128 S. Ct. 2678 (2008).

10. An excellent example of our overreaching and irrational criminal justice system is *State v. Smith*, 2010 WI 16, which required a seventeen-year-old boy to register as a sex offender even though he was never convicted, *or even accused*, of a sex crime. The reason was that the majority of the justices *rejected* the boy's argument "that the purpose of the sex offender registry is to protect the public from sex offenders." Two justices, to their credit, dissented from the majority's nonsensical opinion. See Michael D. Cicchini, "Sex Offender Registries: They're Not Just for Sex Offenders Anymore," the Legal Watchdog, December 4, 2010, at thelegalwatchdog.blogspot.com/2010/12/sex-offender-registries-theyre-not-just.html (accessed November 6, 2011).

Chapter One

"How the Hell Did I Wind Up Here?"

Just yesterday you had a great family, a decent job, and some money in the bank. You also had innumerable freedoms and luxuries that you took entirely for granted, as most of us do. You were free to come and go as you pleased. You were largely free to do whatever you wanted and to see whomever you wanted. Life was good. No, life was *great*, but you didn't even realize it. Until today.

Today you woke up, like millions of other citizens, as a convicted criminal. You didn't rob anyone or do anything else that most people would consider seriously wrong. You may not have even known that what you *did* do could be considered a criminal act at all. Perhaps you were just arguing with your spouse, and you ended up convicted of disorderly conduct as a domestic-abuse crime. Or perhaps you were just disciplining your child; all you did was spank him, and there weren't even any injuries, but you ended up convicted of felony child abuse. Maybe you just had three or four beers at a cookout and drove home, and you ended up convicted not only of drunk driving, but also of felony reckless endangerment of safety.

Regardless of what you did, and regardless of what you were ultimately convicted of—which often are two entirely different things—maybe you're now serving a prison sentence. If you're lucky, you're only serving a short jail term, or maybe you've even avoided incarceration altogether, at least for now. In any case, you'll have to deal with the numerous and serious consequences that go along with a conviction, some of which you don't even know about yet.

For example, if you were convicted of a domestic abuse–related crime, even if the victim suffered no physical injury at all, you may never be able to possess a firearm again—not for hunting, for sport, or even for protection.[1] If you were convicted of certain crimes involving controlled substances, you

1

may be disqualified from several government programs, including federal student loans and other government benefits. [2] If you were convicted of drunk driving, your driving privileges will be revoked or at least severely limited. If you were convicted of any felony crime—a feat the government can accomplish more easily than you think—you might not be allowed to vote in any election, possibly for many years to come. [3] If you are not a United States citizen and were convicted of any felony crime, or even one of the many qualifying misdemeanor crimes, you might very well be deported. [4] Perhaps most surprisingly, if you were convicted of a crime, you may be required to register as a sex offender—even if you were never convicted, *or even accused*, of a sex crime. [5]

Regardless of whether you served prison time, jail time, or no time, you're very likely to have probation, parole or some other type of supervision, often for years to come. That supervision will dramatically limit where you can go and what you can do. [6] If you were convicted of a domestic-abuse or child-abuse crime, your supervising agent may prevent you from having any contact with your spouse, your children, or others whom you love. Regardless of the crime of which you were convicted, you may lose your job; or, if you work out of state, you may be forced to quit because your agent won't let you cross state lines. The agent will also dictate where and with whom you may live. Alcohol will likely be forbidden under any supervision scheme; no more wine with dinner or even a cold beer on a hot summer day. And if you're caught violating any of these rules, your agent can revoke your supervision and you'll likely be returned, or sent for the first time, to jail or prison.

Finally, you're also out a great deal of money. You had to pay thousands of dollars in attorney's fees, maybe a fine, and definitely court costs, including numerous bureaucratic surcharges that you'd never even heard of before. (Criminal justice is a big business and needs to be funded.) To add insult to injury, you will even have to pay the government for the privilege of having an agent supervise you on probation or parole. The consequences of your conviction are staggering and seemingly limitless. Your life may never be the same.

As this new reality starts to soak in, you ask yourself this question: "How the hell did I wind up here?" The answer may very well be this: Somewhere along your meandering path through the criminal justice system, your constitutional rights were ignored, circumvented, or flat-out destroyed.

■ ■ ■

Before going any further, let me backtrack a bit and change the context of the question. "How the hell did *I* wind up here?" More specifically, how did I, the author, wind up being a criminal defense lawyer, and, even more specifically than that, what could possibly inspire me to sit here late on a weeknight, tired and bleary-eyed, pounding out the first chapter of this book? The answers to these questions will provide you with some background and context for later chapters.

Not long ago, I would probably have been labeled a corporate type, and maybe even a Republican. I had voted for George Bush (Senior, not Junior). I had earned my MBA degree from Marquette University, and even passed the CPA examination on my first try. I was employed in the corporate world but, quite frankly, found the particular jobs that I held to be boring and not terribly significant in any imaginable sense of the word. Given that I was still (relatively) young and I was searching for something a bit more substantial for my life's work, I decided to study law. In 1997 I enrolled, once again, at Marquette University, but this time just a block or two east down Wisconsin Avenue, on the edge of campus at the law school.[7]

During law school I found the law to be so entertaining and, with the exception of patent law, so easy that I did exceptionally well, and I earned multiple awards and honors along the way to graduating in only two and one-half years. With that, and the then-booming economy, came job offers. I received offers from all of the firms in Milwaukee to which I applied, and accepted a job with a large, national law firm where I practiced real-estate law, commercial litigation, and some corporate bankruptcy law. I had finally arrived. I now had more than just a job. I was a professional (licensed and all) and had an actual career.

As you might guess, however, new associates in large, national law firms don't often get to do what is commonly thought of as lawyers' work. Lawyers' work—for example, consulting with clients, appearing in court, arguing motions, and trying cases—is typically reserved for the partners or, in some cases, the senior associates. The new associates, on the other hand, are often left to sift through boxes of documents, read and summarize seemingly endless and badly worded contractual fine print, or, if they're lucky, research and write legal memorandums on arcane, but sometimes interesting, legal issues. This situation was not unique to the law firm where I worked. By necessity, it's just the way that big firms operate, and doing it any other way wouldn't make economic sense.

As a result, I found myself once again feeling somewhat insubstantial and unfulfilled. I certainly had nothing against representing rich people or giant corporations. In fact, I hoped to someday be one (a rich person), or possibly run one (a giant corporation). However, my career was starting to feel an awful lot like the corporate jobs that I held before I went to law school. It was, once again, time for a change. After surprisingly little thought, I decided that I would open my very own law office. I wanted to *really* practice law. I wanted to do lawyers' work.

In January of 2002, I took the plunge. I rented an office, hung out my shingle, and opened my practice.[8] I still remember standing in my then-empty office while my brother painted the walls and my mother arranged the furniture placement. I had already made plans for phone service and other necessary office-related items. I even had a budget and something that loosely resembled a business plan. Things were really falling into place, and I was finally going to be a "real lawyer."

There was, however, one not-so-insignificant problem: all of the legal areas in which I wanted to practice required some experience in the courtroom, and I had none. Yes, I could research and write a legal brief with the best of them.[9] Yes, I believed I could argue the law, if pressed. Yes, I'd even taken a trial-advocacy class in law school, where we stood up in front of our classmates and practiced our opening statements and closing arguments. But none of this was enough. If my plan was to work, if my law practice was really going to happen, I needed some actual courtroom experience. Enter criminal-defense work.

■ ■ ■

When a person is accused of a crime and cannot afford an attorney, the law says that the state must appoint one.[10] Indigent individuals accused of crimes are usually represented by one of the state's public-defender offices. State public-defender offices, however, often employ far fewer public-defender attorneys than what is actually needed to handle their caseload. As a result, an office may farm out cases to lawyers in private practice within the local community.[11] These lawyers, collectively known as the private bar, represent some of the indigent clients and, when a case is completed, send a bill to the public defender's office. The hourly rate paid by the public defender's office is usually far less than the going market rate for attorneys. In some states, it's only a small fraction of the going rate. But when you're starting your own practice and need courtroom experience, it's an excellent opportunity.

I soon learned that the state public defender's branch office for my county—an office that literally sat on the same block as my law office—had a lot of cases to farm out, but not many private-bar attorneys willing to work at the rate of pay that they offered.[12] This, of course, meant that there were a lot of available cases for me. These cases would get me into the courtroom to argue and, if I was incredibly lucky, maybe even have a jury trial—exactly the experience I needed to launch my own private practice.

This would be perfect for a few months, or maybe even a year. Granted, I didn't know much about criminal law and procedure, and I knew even less about constitutional rights, but I knew I could do it. First, as I kept trying to convince myself, I was smart and could learn. Second, in reality, the job of a criminal-defense lawyer would probably be nothing more than a mere formality anyway, right? Even if the police happened to botch the job and arrest the wrong person, there's no way a prosecutor would actually prosecute an innocent man or woman, is there? We were taught in law school that the prosecutor doesn't just pursue convictions. Rather, the prosecutor takes on a dual role: he or she is both an advocate for the state *and* a so-called "minister of justice."[13] In other words, the prosecutor would be mindful of the defendant's rights as well. After all, everyone in society suffers when the rights of any of our citizens are violated, or when one of us is wrongly convicted.

On top of that, there is the judge—the neutral and detached magistrate, sworn and dedicated to dispassionately applying the rule of law and protecting individual rights. And besides, even if prosecutors and judges weren't always this idealistic, surely, as a matter of self-interest, they would not want to risk the wrongful conviction of a citizen. Defendants have numerous rights of appeal, and the error-correcting appellate courts would be hovering above, no doubt chomping at the bit to stamp out any injustice that might happen to slip through. At least that's how I thought the system worked.

The important point for now, however, is that I did not enter into criminal-defense work with some ax to grind against the government; in fact, I had a very high, even naive opinion about police, prosecutors, judges, and the system. I expected criminal law to be almost collaborative, with the common goal being a reasonable resolution or, when necessary, a fair trial, with all close calls on legal issues being resolved in favor of the defendant. "[I]t is far worse to convict an innocent man than to let a guilty man go free," right?[14] I expected an atmosphere of collegiality, professionalism, and respect. I expected law-abiding police—stories about crooked cops seemed to be within the domain of Hollywood, not of reality—and reasonable prosecutors and judges, all of whom would respect constitutional rights.

Nor did I enter into criminal-defense work with any love of the indigent, or in support of any social cause whatsoever. In fact, I was an attorney with an MBA, a CPA, and a business background. I was in this for purely selfish reasons. I was just looking to gain a little courtroom experience so I could launch my career in other practice areas. In other words, I entered the criminal-defense profession as a fair-minded, dispassionate, and unbiased participant. I also entered naively, giving the benefit of the doubt by assuming that others in the criminal justice system would be equally fair-minded, unbiased, and, if not dispassionate, at least reasonable.

What I found, however, was unpleasantly surprising, to say the least. I found that in many cases the police, prosecutors, and judges were the ones with the common goal, but that goal was to bypass, not to enforce, our constitutional rights. Some prosecutors and some judges—unable to cloak their disgust for the Constitution and the procedural rule of law—would even openly mock and ridicule defendants, defense lawyers, and the criminal process. In some cases, the hostility directed at defendants and defense counsel was incredibly intense and highly uncomfortable. It was beyond adversarial. It was flat-out unprofessional.

As my disbelief grew with every new case that I handled, I quickly realized that what was intended to be a temporary layover in the world of criminal defense was fast becoming a permanent career. Today, many years after opening my own office and accepting my first criminal case, I not only continue to practice criminal law, but I have practiced *only* criminal law and have declined to represent clients in any other type of case. My study and practice of criminal law has consumed all of my working hours, routinely extending into the nights and weekends.

But I didn't stop there. In order to vent about the things that I witnessed on a weekly basis, I began to write about criminal law. I wrote about how police, prosecutors, and judges violate the rules, and how the law should be changed to stop them. This provided a much-needed outlet for the frustrations caused by some of the judges and other government agents I encountered in my legal practice. My writing—which was well researched, detailed and thorough, rather than amounting to mere opinion pieces—was intended primarily for those in the legal community, and was published in what are called law reviews or law journals. These are scholarly publications that are reserved primarily for articles written by law professors—although judges and practitioners publish in them as well, but to a much lesser extent.

My publication record in only a few years was of such quantity and quality (based on the imperfect but generally accepted yardstick of the institutional prestige of the journals) that it would have earned me tenure a couple of times over had I been a professor at any law school in the country. [15] And I was doing all of this on top of a more than full-time criminal-defense practice. In short, I was sucked in. The craziness and irrationality that I witnessed had me pulled in, hook, line, and sinker. Criminal defense was consuming nearly my every moment. When I wasn't practicing law, I was writing about the law. And when I wasn't writing about the law, I was droning on about the law to anyone who would listen. And when I wasn't droning on about the law, I was having nagging dreams about my criminal cases and what the government was trying to do to my clients.

But shouldn't that be enough? Why, on top of all of this, would I write this book? In short, there was one particular incident that nudged me over the edge of the metaphorical cliff. I had filed a pretrial motion on behalf of a client, asking the judge to exclude a piece of evidence that was not only illegally obtained by the police, but was also highly unreliable with regard to the ultimate issue of my client's guilt or innocence. When I filed this motion I was several years into my career, and, by that time, I had come to expect that most judges would rule against me. However, this motion was so strong that I was cautiously optimistic that the judge would rule in my favor. Even the prosecutor told me privately, before the hearing, that although the judge *should* rule in my favor, he (the prosecutor) was still going to take his shot just to see what happened—so much for the prosecutor's "minister of justice" role.

After the hearing was over, the judge denied my motion and ruled for the prosecutor. In other words, the judge decided that the prosecutor *could* use the piece of evidence at the defendant's trial. But I had been around the block more than a few times and had braced myself for this outcome, so I really wasn't terribly upset. Besides, even though the prosecutor could now use this evidence at trial, it was still very *unreliable* evidence—a point I was confident the jury would recognize. So, all in all, the ruling didn't sink our case.

After the hearing, I went back to my office and went about my business as usual. As the afternoon passed and evening arrived, I was still fine. But then, later that night when I finally went to bed and tried to sleep, the judge's ruling unexpectedly crept back into my mind and started to gnaw at me. The ruling was so contrary to both law and logic—and had been delivered from the judicial pulpit with equal parts arrogance and ignorance—that my frustration and anger slowly began to build. I tried to suppress these emotions and focus on getting to sleep. So I tried to think about other things. Then I tried to read a book. Nothing worked.

Soon I realized that I had tossed and turned for so long that I was due in court again in only a few hours. At this point, given the time and my frustration level, I knew that even a partial night's sleep was out of the question. That was my tipping point. Since I couldn't get the judge or the ruling out of my head, I decided to do something about it. That's when I got up and began to organize my thoughts. I decided then and there, at about 4:00 a.m. on a weekday with no sleep—generally not a good time to be making decisions of any kind—that I had to write this book. I had to go beyond the law reviews and the law journals—publications that are usually read only by law students and law professors. I had to do more. I had to reach a broader audience. I had to write for the person that some lawyers and law-school professors pretentiously refer to as "the non-lawyer."[16]

I hope that you find this book was worth the effort.

NOTES

1. "Misdemeanor Crimes of Domestic Violence and Federal Firearms Prohibitions," Bureau of Alcohol, Firearms, Tobacco and Explosives, at www.atf.gov/publications/download/i/atf-i-3310-3.pdf (accessed March 21, 2010).

2. "Free Application for Federal Student Aid," at www.fafsa.ed.gov/faq003.htm (accessed March 21, 2010).

3. For an overview of, and links to, the various state laws, see "State Felon Voting Laws," at felonvoting.procon.org/view.resource.php?resourceID=000286 (accessed March 21, 2010).

4. "Conviction May Mean Deportation or Removal from U.S.," at criminal.lawyers.com/Conviction-May-Mean-Deportation-or-Removal-from-US.html (accessed March 21, 2010).

5. *State v. Smith*, 2010 WI 16. In this case, the court rejected the defendant's argument "that the purpose of the sex offender registry is to protect the public from sex offenders," and instead made him register for a crime that never involved sex in any way, shape, or form. See Michael D. Cicchini, "Sex Offender Registries: They're Not Just For Sex Offenders Anymore," the Legal Watchdog, December 4, 2010, at thelegalwatchdog.blogspot.com/2010/12/sex-offender-registries-theyre-not-just.html (accessed November 6, 2011).

6. Each person under supervision—whether probation, parole, or extended supervision—will be given a set of rules by his or her agent. For an example of a set of rules, see "Conditions of Probation," Clackamas County (OR), at www.clackamas.us/corrections/info.htm (accessed November 1, 2011). Many of these rules will apply regardless of the crime for which the person is being supervised, while others are specific to the type of crime.

7. When I attended Marquette University Law School, it was located in cozy Sensenbrenner Hall on Wisconsin Avenue. However, it has since moved immediately south to the $81 million Ray and Kay Eckstein Hall, which is now probably the best law-school building in the country. The building was named after the Ecksteins, both Marquette University alums, for their $51 million contribution. See "Ray & Kay Eckstein Hall Campaign," at law.marquette.edu/marquette-lawyers/ray-kay-eckstein-hall-campaign (accessed October 30, 2011).

8. Cicchini Law Office LLC, at www.cicchinilaw.com (accessed March 21, 2010).

9. I remain confident in this claim despite a local judge's statement to a convicted murderer at sentencing that he (the convicted murderer) "can write a brief better than most attorneys in this town." Jessica Stephen, "Miller Gets Life Term, No Parole," *Kenosha (WI) News*, November 12, 2011.

10. *Gideon v. Wainwright*, 372 U.S. 335 (1963). However, like many constitutional rights, this theoretical right to counsel often goes unfulfilled. See Erik Eckholm, "Citing Workload, Public Lawyers Reject New Cases," *New York Times*, November 8, 2008, at www.nytimes.com/2008/11/09/us/09defender.html (accessed March 21, 2010).

11. For example, see the Wisconsin State Public Defender's Office website, at www.wisspd.org/htm/acd/acd.asp (accessed October 30, 2011).

12. Interestingly, the economics of the legal profession changed drastically from the time I started my law practice. By the end of my first decade as a criminal-defense lawyer, the balance of economic power had shifted. Even though the rate of pay for a public-defender appointment remained unchanged at $40 per hour, the number of attorneys ready and willing to accept the appointments had grown dramatically.

13. The vast majority of criminal prosecutions are state cases, not federal cases. State prosecutors are subject to state rules of professional conduct. For an example of a state's rules governing a prosecutor's dual role as both advocate and minister of justice, see Wisconsin Supreme Court rule 20:3.8 and its accompanying American Bar Association comment, at www.wicourts.gov/sc/scrule/DisplayDocument.pdf?content=pdf&seqNo=45324 (accessed March 20, 2010).

14. *In re Winship*, 397 U.S. 358, 372 (1970).

15.   For a free copy of these publications, see "Articles," at cicchinilaw.com/Articles.htm (accessed March 21, 2010). These publications include articles on the exclusionary rule, show-up identifications, the confrontation clause, false confessions, plea bargaining, and prosecutorial misconduct at trial.

16.   The highly entertaining law professor J. Gordon Hylton (law.marquette.edu/faculty-and-staff-directory/detail/2000669) raised this point in the "Lawyer in American Society" class at Marquette University Law School in the fall of 1997. He pointed out how law professors, lawyers, and even law students typically refer to the rest of the world as "non-lawyers," and then challenged us to think of any other profession that divides the world up in such an egocentric way.

Chapter Two

The Nature of Constitutional Rights

The law can be categorized in numerous ways. For example, law can be civil or criminal, procedural or substantive, or federal or state, to name only a few of the available classifications. However, in order to understand the nature of constitutional rights—the hallmark and foundation of criminal law—it is necessary to explain a different type of distinction.

For our purposes, it is helpful to distinguish between what I will call, for the sake of simplicity, a "hard law" and a "soft law." A hard law is a law that is clear-cut, immutable, and subject to little if any real discretion in its application. Conversely, a soft law is a law that is vague, malleable, and subject to a tremendous amount of discretion under a facts-and-circumstances type of analysis. An example will make this distinction very clear.

Suppose Johnny is a seventeen-year-old high-school student. One Friday night Johnny somehow wrangles an invitation to a local college party. Being the "good kid" that he is, he doesn't drink any alcohol and just goes to meet some people—hopefully girls. Johnny can't believe his luck when he meets a cute, friendly, and drunk eighteen-year-old college girl named Jenny, with whom he really hits it off. Johnny and Jenny talk all night, and then things take a romantic turn—something not uncommon for young adults, or, in Johnny's case, older teens. However, as we've already established, Johnny is a "good kid." There is kissing and some touching, but Johnny and Jenny stop there. The pair exchange phone numbers and agree to go out for pizza when Jenny is done studying for college midterms.

The next day, however, there's a knock on Johnny's front door. His parents are still at work, but Johnny answers it. It's the police. They want to ask him some questions because Jenny's parents interrogated their drunken daughter, found out what she was up to last night, and are now alleging that she was sexually assaulted. (They believe that their little Jenny doesn't willingly drink alcohol and fool around with boys, so someone needs to be blamed for this.) Johnny is panicked. His heart is racing. But he decides to answer the officers' questions, for several reasons. First, he's never been in any trouble or had any police contact, so he doesn't even know that he has a choice in the matter. Second, he's always been taught that the police are good and are there to help him, so he really doesn't think he has anything to fear. (The police start this indoctrination early—remember Deputy Friendly back in grade school?) Third, and most importantly, he didn't do anything wrong—in fact, his behavior was quite restrained as hormone-ravaged teenagers go—so he has nothing at all to hide. His innocence will set him free.

Johnny answers the questions, and tells the police that he didn't sexually assault Jenny; it was all consensual. He also tells the police there wasn't even any sex, just touching, and that nothing really happened. After some more follow-up questions, Johnny explains in more detail what he means by "touching." (Let's just say that some clothing was removed.) Then, in the scariest moment of Johnny's young life, the police handcuff him and take him downtown for booking. He'll be held on a cash bail and may not see his home for a long time, but that's actually the least of his worries.

Unfortunately for our not-so-hypothetical Johnny, he just unwittingly confessed to one of the most serious crimes of which a person can be convicted in our country: second-degree sexual assault of a child.[1] This crime could expose him to a possible forty years of incarceration, with subsequent sex-offender reporting, sex-offender supervision, and a host of so-called collateral consequences so severe that it would take a whole chapter just to begin to explain their life-ruining impact.

How did this happen? Well, Johnny just ran up against a classic example of what I've labeled a hard law. It's designed to work to his disadvantage, and, once ensnared, there is no way out. Allow the arresting police officer to explain further, in the following hypothetical dialogue that takes place as he arrests Johnny.

Johnny: But wait, officer, everything was consensual!

Officer: We know you didn't do anything against her will, Johnny. We didn't believe Jenny's parents when they accused you of *that*. But that's not what I meant when I said "assault." You see, Jenny was actually only *fifteen*. Sure, fifteen and eleven months, but still not quite sixteen. That makes this a felony sexual assault in this state. Our law says that someone her age is not capable of legal consent.

Johnny: But she said she was eighteen! I have witnesses.

Officer: Sorry, Johnny. It doesn't matter if you have a dozen witnesses or even if she showed you a fake ID. A mistake, or even a misrepresentation, about the victim's age is not a defense to this crime—at least not in this state.

Johnny: But I'm only seventeen! I'm not even an adult yet. How can you arrest me and charge me with a crime?

Officer: Well, in this state, even though you can't drink, buy cigarettes, or enter into a legally binding contract due to your age, you are considered an adult for criminal law purposes.

Johnny: But how can this be a sex crime? We never even had sex. We just touched each other.

Officer: Oh, that is a tough one, Johnny. But first, even sexual touching is a crime. And second, unfortunately for you, the legislature in this state has decided to define *sexual intercourse* as "any intrusion, however slight, of any part of a person's body (including a hand) into the genital opening of another."[2] I know that's quite wordy, and it's not how normal people define the term *intercourse*; but hey, you elected the representatives in the legislature.

Johnny: No I didn't! I'm only seventeen-years-old. I can't even vote yet.

Officer: Okay. Good point on that one. But you're still going to jail.

Do you get the picture by this point? This sexual-assault law is a hard law because it is clear-cut and immutable. If a seventeen-year-old boy even touches a nearly-sixteen-year-old girl (or vice versa) in a sexual manner, it is a felony sexual assault of a child. Period. There is no facts-and-circumstances analysis. It doesn't matter how old she looked, or if she lied about her age, or even if she consented (because our legal fiction states that she is not capable of consent).[3] And it especially doesn't matter that any reasonable person would conclude either that the real victim was Johnny, not Jenny, or that no crime was even committed, as this is perfectly normal (or even constrained) teenage behavior.

If you have any doubts about whether this type of arrest and prosecution actually happens, I and nearly every defense lawyer I know could think of a very long list of young defendants and their families whose lives have been ruined by the sexual assault of a child law, or the sex-offender registry. In fact, amazingly, the sex-offender registry in some states has expanded to include people who have never even been accused, let alone convicted, of a sex crime.[4] But that is a story for another book.

If you wanted to turn this unjust hard law into a fair and just soft law, how would you do it? You might make criminal liability turn on the facts and circumstances of the case. For example, you might make Jenny's misrepresentation of age a defense for Johnny, provided that his belief that she was eighteen was a reasonable one.[5] You might look to the age difference between the two to determine whether the crime should be a felony or a misdemeanor. You might consider whether there was *actual* intercourse—rather than the legislature's tortured definition of the word—to decide whether there was even a crime at all. These are all facts and circumstances that, if you wanted to turn the sexual assault of a child law into a soft law, would bear on whether there was a criminal offense, how severe it was, and whether there were any defenses to it.

But wait, none of that stuff matters, you're thinking. Regardless of whether this sex-crime law is a hard law or a soft law, Johnny has rights too, and constitutional rights at that. And in this case, his rights were no doubt violated. Most notably, the police never advised Johnny of his right to remain silent; they never read him his *Miranda* warnings. His confession would not be admissible at trial, and without that, all they have is Jenny's accusation, right?

Well, aside from the fact that corroborating evidence is *not* required to convict a person of a felony, what the police did was perfectly legal. Although this is the subject of chapter 4, I'll let the cat out of the bag right now. The right to remain silent, along with nearly every other constitutional right, is a soft law. That means that, unlike the sexual assault of a child law, the right to remain silent is vague, malleable, and subject to manipulation by police, prosecutors, and judges. This allows the police, prosecutors, and judges to simply create the facts and circumstances they need to bypass the constitutional right that might otherwise protect the defendant.

In this case, getting Johnny's confession without reading him his rights was—both figuratively and literally, due to Johnny's age—child's play. By questioning Johnny before his arrest, and at his home, the police were able to skip the *Miranda* warning altogether.[6] Under these facts and circumstances, Johnny was not in custody, and the police were merely investigating a possible crime, rather than interrogating a suspect. Therefore, *Miranda* does not apply. It doesn't matter that the police could have arrested him before questioning him, or that they could have first taken him to the police station. And even if they had arrested Johnny first, before questioning him, the police still have numerous other methods to defeat Johnny's constitutional right to remain silent.[7] We'll explore that in more detail in chapter 4.

For now, though, the purpose of this chapter is to distinguish between a hard law and a soft law. The sexual assault of a child law is a hard law. If it were a soft law, defendants would be able to defend by arguing certain facts and circumstances that would negate criminal liability. In other words, they might be able, in some cases, to rightly avoid a felony conviction. State governments—or at least some state governments—do not want that.

Conversely, constitutional rights are soft laws. This allows the police to create the facts and circumstances necessary to circumvent—or, more accurately, destroy—constitutional rights. Even if the police at first commit a tactical error, there will be other opportunities for them to compensate and correct their gaff. If the police are really having a bad day, and somehow completely fail to create the necessary facts and circumstances during their investigation, don't fret. There will be ample opportunity for the prosecutor to come to the rescue and create those facts and circumstances afterward, at the evidentiary hearings in court. (After all, most police-citizen encounters are not videotaped, but rather are recreated after the fact by the police, in court.) If the prosecutor is particularly inept—or particularly ethical—all is still not lost for the government. In that case, the judge can simply step in and decide that those necessary facts and circumstances exist, even when the prosecutor has conceded that they don't exist. This will be explained in more detail in future chapters, each of which will address a specific constitutional right. As we'll soon see, the deck has been stacked, and it's not stacked in favor of the citizenry.

■ ■ ■

I'm well aware that, at this point, many of you may be thinking, who cares? After all, constitutional rights are just technicalities anyway, and a guilty person is guilty, and shouldn't have constitutional rights. Right?

Well, no. First of all, constitutional rights are not technicalities. They are the very building blocks of the freedom that most of us still enjoy. At this point, however, suffice it to say that constitutional rights are probably thought of as technicalities because they are sometimes at direct odds with the substantive criminal law and, in many cases, can help a factually guilty person go free.

Take, for example, the Wisconsin state government, which decided that every citizen who possesses a marijuana cigarette in his or her home is guilty of a crime, and that crime is a felony if it happens to be the citizen's second or subsequent such transgression.[8] However, we citizens don't want the government to have unrestricted access to our homes in order to search for evidence.[9] Therefore, the substantive law (marijuana cigarettes in the home are illegal) conflicts with the right of privacy (the government can't come into our homes to search for marijuana cigarettes). If the police illegally enter a citizen's home and find a marijuana cigarette, and the prosecutor files a criminal case based on those facts, the illegally obtained evidence could be suppressed or excluded.[10] Without any admissible evidence, of course, the case would have to be dismissed. As a result, a factually guilty person goes unpunished.

But why not give constitutional rights only to those people who don't illegally possess marijuana cigarettes? After all, those who possess them are breaking the law, so they shouldn't be allowed to hide behind the Constitution and escape punishment. Well, there's the rub. You don't know who is breaking the law until you violate every citizen's constitutional right to privacy by unlawfully entering their homes to look for the illegal marijuana cigarette. Therefore, the only way for the Constitution to have any teeth is to apply it equally to all citizens. If the "end" (convicting every citizen who possesses a marijuana cigarette) is allowed to justify the "means" (entering all citizens' homes to search for marijuana cigarettes), the Constitution disappears, and we now have a police state. Granted, a police state with no marijuana cigarettes, but a police state just the same. I don't think I'm overstating the case by asserting that this would be an unwelcome state of affairs.

But, surprisingly, as bad as having a police state would be, it's actually not the worst thing that happens when we disregard constitutional safeguards. In many cases, constitutional rights are *not* at odds with the substantive criminal law, as they were in the marijuana cigarette example above. Sometimes, police behavior can violate a person's constitutional rights *and* lead to the conviction of an innocent person *and* result in the guilty person going free.

An excellent example of this is when the police are investigating a crime and use highly suggestive identification procedures—such as single-suspect show-ups, or poorly constructed lineups or photo arrays—in order to "get the bad guy." Such practices not only violate the suspect's constitutional due-process rights, but the identification procedures are so unreliable (yet nonetheless persuasive to jurors) that they often lead to false identifications and wrongful convictions.[11] And further, once that innocent person is convicted, the true perpetrator not only escapes his or her rightful punishment but will remain free to commit more crimes. Everyone loses, and everyone loses big. When the police—and later the prosecutor and the judge—convince themselves that they are doing the "right thing" by bypassing the Constitution, there can be unintended and devastating consequences for the innocent and for the safety of the community.

Finally, aside from whether the Constitution is a mere technicality or not, the numerous protections it affords us throughout the criminal process are desperately needed—even for the factually guilty—to protect us against the ever-expanding power of the government. The reality is that we live in a "tough on crime" environment that has escalated, in many ways, well beyond what is rational or even beneficial for society, and we citizens need all the protection we can get.

For example, our state legislatures add new, far-reaching criminal statutes every year. Each state now has several hundred, if not a thousand or more, different criminal laws to use in its "war" on whatever type of conduct it chooses to target on any given day. (In recent years, for example, the "war on terror" has overshadowed the "war on drugs.") Further, as we'll see in future chapters, the penalties for violating these criminal laws have become both staggering and irrational, even for crimes where there is no direct or indirect harm to anyone, and where the defendant had no criminal intent whatsoever.[12]

Additionally, the police are afforded incredibly broad power in what they can do, and to whom they can do it, during the course of their investigations. Prosecutors have been given unlimited and unchecked discretion in what and whom they can charge. Judges are given free rein to dole out the punishments they see fit, and they're not shy about it either.[13] Although we as a country account for only 5 percent of the world's population, we account for 25 percent of the world's prisoners.[14] Some judges have even created facts out of thin air to justify sending defendants to prison[15] —a topic we'll cover in a later chapter. In short, our government—between all of its various agencies and branches—is downright fanatical when it comes to crime, conviction, and punishment.[16]

In the next chapter, and before we start to get into specific constitutional rights, I will illustrate in greater detail just how easy it is for ordinary citizens, and morally good people, to be accused of a crime and ensnared in our vast, weblike criminal justice system.

NOTES

1. For an example of a second-degree sexual assault of a child law and the definition of the terms *sexual contact* and *sexual intercourse*, see Wisconsin Statutes sections 948.02(2), 948.01(5), and 948.01(6), at www.legis.state.wi.us/statutes/Stat0948.pdf (accessed March 26, 2010).

2. Ibid.

3. For an excellent case discussing the horrific nature of the sexual-assault law, see *State v. Jadowski*, 2004 WI 68, where the defendant was convicted for sexual contact with a minor despite his reasonable but mistaken belief that the minor was nineteen years old. This belief was based on the minor's false representation that she was an adult, as well as her possession of a state-issued, but counterfeit, identification card. Despite this, the court would not allow the defendant to use those facts to defend the sexual-assault allegation.

4. See Michael D. Cicchini, "Sex Offender Registries: They're Not Just for Sex Offenders Anymore," the Legal Watchdog, December 4, 2010, at http://thelegalwatchdog.blogspot.com/2010/12/sex-offender-registries-theyre-not-just.html (accessed November 6, 2011).

5. Some states *do* permit defendants to assert a fraudulent misrepresentation of age defense. See *State v. Jadowski*, 2004 WI 68, ¶ 26, note 20, for a summary.

6. The *Miranda* warning is aptly named after *Miranda v. Arizona*, 384 U.S. 436 (1966). For the right against self-incrimination more generally, see the United States Constitution, Fifth Amendment, at topics.law.cornell.edu/constitution/fifth_amendment (accessed March 26, 2010).

7. For example, it is actually very difficult for a suspect to invoke his or her *Miranda* rights. See Michael D. Cicchini, "The New Miranda Warning," Marquette University Law School Faculty Blog, November 8, 2010, at law.marquette.edu/facultyblog/2010/11/08/the-new-miranda-warning/ (accessed March 12, 2011).

8. Wisconsin Statutes section 961.41(3g)(e), at www.legis.state.wi.us/statutes/Stat0961.pdf (accessed March 26, 2010).

9. United States Constitution, Fourth Amendment, at topics.law.cornell.edu/constitution/fourth_amendment (accessed March 26, 2010).

10. The U.S. Supreme Court, frighteningly, has held that evidence should *rarely* be suppressed (that is, excluded from trial), even in cases of illegal police searches. For more detail, see chapter 5, as well as Michael D. Cicchini, "An Economics Perspective on the Exclusionary Rule and Deterrence," 75 *Missouri Law Review* 459 (2010), available at cicchinilaw.com/Articles.htm (accessed March 8, 2011).

11. For a deeper analysis of false identifications and wrongful convictions, including a survey of the psychological studies on the topic, see Michael D. Cicchini and Joseph Easton, "Reforming the Law on Show-Up Identifications," 100 *Journal of Criminal Law and Criminology* 381 (2010), available at cicchinilaw.com/Articles.htm (accessed March 26, 2010).

12. For a brief but excellent discussion of these issues, see Joel McNally, "Playing on the Public's Fear of Crime," *Cap Times*, March 13, 2010, at host.madison.com/ct/news/opinion/column/joel_mcnally/article_f95572fd-50c1-5800-847c-a2ca738463e1.html (accessed March 26, 2010).

13. Interestingly, the so-called Great Recession of 2009 and its accompanying state-budget shortfalls have actually forced some states, at least temporarily, to be more reasonable on nonviolent and victimless crime, and have tempered some of the incredibly harsh and draconian penalties that lawmakers love to impose. See McNally, "Playing on the Public's Fear of Crime."

14. For an excellent discussion of population figures and incarceration rates, see Adam Liptak, "Inmate Count in U.S. Dwarfs Other Nations'," *New York Times*, April 23, 2008, at www.nytimes.com/2008/04/23/us/23prison.html (accessed March 26, 2010).

15. See Michael D. Cicchini, "Judge Makes Up Facts and Sends Autistic Defendant to Prison," the Legal Watchdog, November 28, 2010, at thelegalwatchdog.blogspot.com/2010/11/judge-makes-up-facts-and-sends-autistic.html (accessed November 6, 2011).

16. Some states are more fanatical than others. For example, despite nearly identical crime rates and demographics, Wisconsin incarcerates more than twice the number of its citizens than does Minnesota. See Michael O'Hear, "Wisconsin v. Minnesota," Life Sentences Blog, May 18, 2011, at www.lifesentencesblog.com/?p=2150 (accessed October 30, 2011).

Chapter Three

"How Can You Defend Those People?"

> We, as criminal defense lawyers, are forced to deal with some of the lowest people on earth, people who have no sense of right and wrong, people who will lie in court to get what they want, people who do not care who gets hurt in the process. It is our job—our sworn duty—as criminal defense lawyers, to protect our clients from these people.[1]

Hopefully the not-so-hypothetical example in chapter 2, regarding Johnny's sexual assault of Jenny, illustrates just how easy it is for good people to get charged with and convicted of serious crimes. However, I realize that this proposition runs contrary to the well-established views of most people. Most of us have our own preconceived notions about the type of person that actually gets caught up in the criminal justice system. Unfortunately, these views have not been shaped by what actually and routinely happens in courtrooms across the country. Rather, our views have been shaped by what we see on television and read in the newspaper. The problem, however, is that what is deemed newsworthy is not what is representative of reality.[2]

In many communities, the people who are routinely investigated and charged with crimes include people like you and me. Criminal defendants include medical doctors, college students, patent-holding inventors, schoolteachers, scientists, graduate students, lawyers, dentists, business executives, public administrators, single parents, college professors, nurses, high-school students, military veterans, artists, grandparents, chefs, pastors, therapists, computer analysts, common laborers, the unemployed, and even—*gasp!*—government agents. No individual is safe from the government's reach. Anyone—regardless of age, sex, race, income, employment, or community status—can find him- or herself charged with a crime.

But again, you might be thinking at this point, so what? People are charged not based on who they are, but what they do. Any type of person is capable of bad acts, and anyone who commits such acts should be prosecuted. And besides, if the newspaper and television are any indication, violent and horrific crime is way up, right?[3]

Well, consider this: If you're running a news program you could, on the one hand, report on the hundreds of cases that were ground through the local courts that day. Most of them would involve domestic arguments, reckless driving, child spankings, neighbor disputes, check bouncing, consensual sex between teens, marijuana possession, and bar scuffles. If you reported on that, you'd certainly be giving your viewers an accurate, representative view of the criminal justice system. Or, on the other hand, you could report on the one or two extraordinary cases—for example, the huge drug operation or the Mafia-like slaying—and get more interest than if you had reported on all of the run-of-the mill cases combined.[4] In fact, if you were to cover the run-of-the-mill cases, either you would be fired, or your news operation wouldn't be in business very long.

The point is that the people who are getting charged with crimes are no different from you and me. More importantly, the things they are doing to get themselves charged—even when charged with serious felonies—are, by and large, not so bad. In many cases, the underlying actions that lead to the criminal charges are no different from the things that you and I have already done. Don't believe me? Consider some of the following examples.

A grandfather is accused of kidnapping a young boy, his grandson. The boy's father (Grandpa's son) had called the police to report the two missing a few hours after Grandpa was supposed to have returned home with the boy. According to the police, Grandpa was actually found with the boy, in his car on the side of road. The car had been traveling in the direction of the boy's home, but had stalled. It turns out that Grandpa was actually heading back to his son's house to drop off the boy, but had car trouble and decided to just wait by the side of the road until help arrived. On top of that, Grandpa lost track of the time, and he had forgotten his cell phone at home, so he didn't receive any of his son's phone calls. When the two were returned safely, the boy's father (Grandpa's son) breathed a sigh of relief and thanked the police for saving the day.

Nice ending, right? Not so quick. Once involved, the state thought it perfectly within its power, and its right, to prosecute Grandpa. This was no longer a family matter. Grandpa was charged with felony kidnapping,[5] incurred thousands of dollars in legal-defense fees, and had dozens of sleepless and anxious nights. Although the defense filed two pretrial motions to dismiss the case on the theory that no crime had been committed, the commissioner and judge refused these requests and denied the motions. After mulling it over, however, the prosecutor ultimately changed his mind. He finally dismissed the case, but only after several months had passed and several thousands of dollars had been incurred by the taxpayers and the defendant.

Consider another example: A woman is accused of criminal extortion. What did she do? Did she get some dirt on her company's CEO and hold it over his head while demanding a quick payday in exchange for her silence? Did she sleep with a married head basketball coach of a major university in hopes of squeezing millions of dollars out of him?[6] Not exactly. Instead, she was home at her condominium one day when she saw a local troublemaker and known juvenile delinquent milling about, looking to cause more trouble. She yelled at him, essentially telling him to get the hell away from her home or she would come out there and beat him silly. The prosecutor alleged language that was a bit more descriptive and graphic; the defendant denied using such language.

But even if the prosecutor's version of events was correct, how can that possibly be extortion? Well, extortion has only two components, or what we lawyers call elements. They are (1) threatening a person with violence (here, "I'll beat you silly," or similar language); and (2) attempting to get the person to do an act against his or her will (here, "get away from my home").[7] It doesn't matter that the juvenile had no business being near the home in the first place, or that he actually claimed to be leaving the property anyway. (This, of course, made the woman's order to leave *consistent* with his will, rather than against it, which meant that this couldn't possibly constitute extortion.) The defense motions to dismiss this nonsense—again based on the theory that, even if the factual allegation was true, no crime had been committed—were denied after the preliminary hearing by the commissioner, and again before trial by the judge. The case was only dismissed months later when the "victim" (the trespassing juvenile delinquent) ignored his state-issued subpoena and refused to show up for trial. It turned out he had better things to do that day than help prosecute this heinous crime that he, himself, had reported.

Here's a domestic example: Consider the mother who got into an argument with her husband and their sixteen-year-old son. She wanted to discipline the son for behavioral problems, but the husband took their son's side. The three argued, and Mom (and Mom alone) was charged with four crimes. Which ones? First, they argued and voices were raised by all, including Mom, which led to a disorderly conduct charge.[8]

Second, the son got in Mom's face and she pushed him back onto the couch. When later taking the son's statement, the police smartly suggested that Mom's push might have "caused him pain." The son was quick to agree, which led to a felony child-abuse charge, rather than misdemeanor battery, because the son was under the age of eighteen.[9]

Third, the son then gave Mom a piece of his mind, and, when he finished, he tried to storm out of the room. Mom grabbed him by the arm and yelled, "Don't talk to me like that!" The son freed himself after a second or two and went to his room, but this led to a felony false-imprisonment charge for the approximately two-second restraint of movement. [10]

Fourth and finally, the husband, looking to gain the son's favor at Mom's expense, went to call the police. Mom grabbed the phone and asked him, "What the hell is wrong with you, getting the police involved like that?" This led to a felony intimidation of a witness charge. [11]

But this is only scratching the surface. Here are some more examples in abbreviated form: *You might find yourself charged with a crime if* . . . you walk out of the house with a pocketknife (carrying a concealed weapon) . . . you yell at your spouse (disorderly conduct as a domestic-abuse crime) . . . you flirt with the cute checkout employee at the local megamart, but only during business hours, and only when you're there to make actual purchases (felony stalking) . . . you unsuccessfully attempt to slap someone's butt (attempted sexual assault) . . . you spank your eight-year-old child, over his clothing, leaving no marks of any kind (felony child abuse) . . .

First, I'm not kidding about any of these examples. Second, I hope by now I've convinced you that anyone can get charged with a crime for virtually anything. And I haven't even addressed the cases where there was, in fact, a real crime with a real victim, but the victim, police, and prosecutor went after the wrong person. Nor have I addressed the myriad of crimes that many people believe shouldn't even be crimes to begin with—for example, a cancer patient smoking marijuana (which is still against the law, and possibly even a felony, in many states); older teens and young adults having consensual sex (contrary to legal fiction, minors *are* capable of consenting to sexual relations); spouses cheating on one another (yes, adultery is still a crime in many states); bouncing a check at the local megamart (sometimes big business is the prosecutor's biggest client); or driving a car with a suspended driver's license (some cities dedicate entire courts to handling their high volume of criminal traffic cases).

What all of these examples are intended to do is demonstrate the incredible importance of constitutional rights. We now know, as this chapter has shown, that governmental power is often exercised quite unreasonably and arbitrarily. This happens in the context of deciding who gets charged, what crimes they're charged with, how severely they're punished if convicted, and even what types of postpunishment schemes we concoct to haunt them for the balance of their lives. In fact, in many cases, the only thing standing between us and this tremendous, arbitrary governmental power is the Constitution. If our constitutional rights are not strong, and if we cannot rely on them for our protection, then we may fall victim to the government's irrational and life-ruining "war on crime," or its overreaching but politically popular "tough on crime" crusade.

■ ■ ■

If I have done my job, you will now have a newfound appreciation for—or at the very least, a curiosity about—our individual constitutional rights. The Constitution serves as the foundation of our very freedom and, more specifically, protects us from the ever-expanding reach of the government. This includes the state-legislatures-gone-wild—which produce new criminal laws much like a factory churns out consumer products—as well as the police, prosecutors, and, yes, even the judges.

Further, I also hope that I've convinced you of the importance of ensuring that each and every one of us—even those initially perceived to be factually guilty—is afforded his or her Constitutional rights. This is important for several reasons. First, as illustrated in the marijuana-cigarette example from chapter 2, it is impossible to selectively enforce the Constitution only for the factually innocent; rather, if the Constitution is to protect anyone, it must protect everyone. Second, in many cases, such as the suggestive, single-person show-up identification procedure, constitutional violations can actually lead to wrongful convictions of the factually innocent. Third, despite the arrogance of some government agents, they don't *know* who is really factually guilty or factually innocent. And fourth, the term factually guilty, as used in the criminal justice system, often does not equate to moral or ethical guilt in the real world. Consequently, it is critical that everyone, without exception, be afforded the same constitutional guarantees in every single case.

With that settled, it is now time to get to business. In the chapters that follow, I will discuss specific constitutional rights and revisit the concept of the soft law that was first introduced in chapter 2. In so doing, I will show you precisely how some of our police, prosecutors, and judges go about destroying each of our individual constitutional rights.

Welcome to the world of constitutional criminal law.

NOTES

1. Defense lawyers widely attribute this quote to Cynthia Roseberry. See, for example, Law Offices of Lanhon Odom, at www.dentoncriminaldefenseattorney.com/; the Cure Law Office, at thecurelawoffice.com/; Law Office of Alfred McDonald, PC, at www.arizonadefender.com/about.htm; Constance A. Camus, Maryland Trial Lawyer, at mary-

landtriallawyer.net/legal-services/criminal-defense-services/; Criminal Lawyers in New Jersey, at www.marainlaw.com/page.php?here=quotations; and House Law Office, at jshouselaw.com/default.aspx (all accessed October 30, 2011).

2. Joel McNally, "Playing on the Public's Fear of Crime," *Cap Times*, March 13, 2010, at host.madison.com/ct/news/opinion/column/joel_mcnally/article_f95572fd-50c1-5800-847c-a2ca738463e1.html (accessed March 26, 2010).

3. See McNally, "Playing on the Public's Fear of Crime."

4. I learned firsthand another media practice: report on all salacious allegations, but then when the allegations fall apart and the criminal case is dismissed, simply drop the story. That is, don't update your viewers or readers because the facts, once discovered, are no longer newsworthy. To learn more about my experience with the media, see Michael D. Cicchini, "On the Media: Milwaukee Journalists Fail Miserably; Kudos to Kenosha News," May 30, 2011, the Legal Watchdog, at thelegalwatchdog.blogspot.com/2011/05/on-media-milwaukee-journalists-fail.html (accessed October 30, 2011).

5. For an example of a felony kidnapping–type charge that requires only that the defendant kept the child out past the time that the parent expected the child to be returned, see Wisconsin Statute section 948.31 (2), at legis.wisconsin.gov/statutes/Stat0948.pdf (accessed March 12, 2011).

6. See "Karen Cunagin Sypher Found Guilty," ESPN Men's Basketball, August 6, 2010, at http://sports.espn.go.com/ncb/news/story?id=5440210 (accessed March 8, 2011).

7. For an example of an extortion charge, see Wisconsin Statute section 943.30, at legis.wisconsin.gov/statutes/Stat0943.pdf (accessed March 12, 2011).

8. For an example of a disorderly-conduct charge, see Wisconsin Statute section 947.01, at legis.wisconsin.gov/statutes/Stat0947.pdf (accessed March 12, 2011).

9. For an example of a felony child-abuse charge, see Wisconsin Statute section 948.03, at legis.wisconsin.gov/statutes/Stat0948.pdf (accessed March 12, 2011).

10. For an example of a felony false-imprisonment charge, see Wisconsin Statute section 940.30, at legis.wisconsin.gov/statutes/Stat0940.pdf (accessed March 12, 2011).

11. For an example of a felony intimidation of a witness charge, see Wisconsin Statute section 940.43.

Chapter Four

Self-Incrimination

You (Sort of) Have the Right to Remain Silent

Probably the most well-known constitutional right is the Fifth Amendment right against self-incrimination.[1] We've heard the now-famous *Miranda* warning dozens of times on police television dramas. When the hero cop finally cracks the case near the end of the episode and arrests the bad guy, he or she sternly utters those familiar words, just as the scene fades to commercial: "You have the right to remain silent; anything you say can and will be used against you in a court of law . . ."

In reality, however, *Miranda* warnings are not used that way. In fact, many cases are built around only a single, unsubstantiated (and often ridiculous) allegation of wrongdoing, with no supporting physical evidence whatsoever. In these instances, the police *need* a self-incriminating statement, or confession, in order to strengthen the criminal allegation for the prosecutor's office. Therefore, the police are not so quick to suggest to a suspect that he or she "remain silent." If the suspect were to do so, there might not even be a prosecution, let alone a conviction.

Fortunately for the police, however, the constitutional right against self-incrimination is a soft law. As a result, the police, with the help of prosecutors and judges, have been able to develop numerous techniques to legally avoid giving *Miranda* warnings altogether. Further, in instances where they have to give *Miranda* warnings, they are very adept at convincing the suspect to waive, or give up, the right to remain silent and even the right to an attorney. Finally, if the police are not able to obtain a statement within the incredibly broad parameters set for them under the law, the judge, at the pretrial evidentiary hearing, can simply bail the police out and save the day for the prosecutor.

■ ■ ■

First things first: What exactly are *Miranda* warnings? *Miranda* warnings consist of the police or other government agents informing suspects that (1) they have the right to remain silent; (2) any statements they make may be used in evidence against them; (3) they have the right to have an attorney present before or during questioning; and (4) if they cannot afford an attorney, they have the right to ask the court to appoint one before they are interrogated.[2]

As a preliminary matter, just how useful are these warnings to begin with? After reading them, you might have more questions than answers. You might wonder what would happen if you remained silent. Could your *silence* be used against you in evidence? Conversely, what if you asked for an attorney? Is that request a "statement" that can be used against you in evidence? Finally, do you get the attorney only if you agree to make a statement, or can you get an attorney and still remain silent?

As you can now see, the actual usefulness of these warnings is certainly open to debate. I would venture that even many attorneys don't know the answers to some of these questions. In fact, the answers are not necessarily straightforward. As a *general* rule, however, a suspect's post-*Miranda* request for an attorney may not be used against him or her in court, although a plain reading of the warnings seems to suggest otherwise. The other questions, unfortunately, are not so easily answered.[3]

In any case, let's assume that you are a suspect in a crime. The police know that if they were to read you these warnings, you might actually exercise your right to remain silent and refuse to talk to them. The police do not want this. Remember, this may well be a situation where they need your incriminating statement, or the prosecutor won't have a strong case, or any case at all. Therefore, the simplest way for the police to solve this problem, before it even becomes a problem, is to simply avoid giving you the *Miranda* warnings in the first place.

Contrary to what many people think, the police don't have to read you the warnings unless two things are true: (1) you are in custody; *and* (2) the police are interrogating you. We lawyers call this custodial interrogation.[4] The easiest way for the police to avoid custodial interrogation is to interrogate first, and arrest second. If you're not technically arrested at the time the police are interrogating you, then you are *not* in custody, and they can interrogate you for as long as they want without any *Miranda* warnings.

How can the police accomplish this? It's quite easy for them, actually. All they have to do is take advantage of our ignorance of the law. Most people don't know they can simply refuse to talk to police or, in some cases, even walk away from the police. (After all, if people actually knew that, we wouldn't need *Miranda* warnings.) Police understand this; therefore, they may simply approach you at your home and start questioning you before they arrest you, like they did to our not-so-hypothetical Johnny in chapter 2. The police may also approach you at work or any other place from which you are unlikely to simply walk away. The police know that in these places you will be caught off guard and will likely talk to them.

The police may also call you on the phone and tell you that it's important to meet right away, for some unspecified reason, and that you should "voluntarily" come to the police station. This is an even easier, but slightly riskier, strategy for them. If you're alert enough, you may contact a lawyer who would tell you not to go. (Surprisingly, though, not all lawyers are that astute.) However, if you choose to accept their invitation and go to the police station, you would probably not be considered under arrest, and the police could legally interrogate you without *Miranda* warnings. In fact, in one published court case, a seventeen-year-old suspect was interrogated by the police at the police station for two hours. His parents were prevented from seeing him, and he was never told that he was free to leave. Even under these circumstances, the court held that the suspect was not in custody—because a hypothetical, reasonable person in his position would supposedly have felt free to leave at any time—and therefore the police did not violate his rights when they failed to read him his *Miranda* warnings.[5]

In some cases, however, the police may choose to arrest you first, for a variety of reasons. In these cases, they can still avoid *Miranda* warnings by making sure that you are technically not interrogated. Remember, only custodial interrogation triggers *Miranda*. Mere arrest (custody) or questioning (interrogation) alone is not enough; both are needed. Therefore, if the police arrest you and, instead of *asking* you things, they *tell* you things, the judge might not consider that to be an interrogation, and the police could again avoid *Miranda* warnings altogether.[6]

For example, consider the sexual assault of a child example in chapter 2, where Johnny had consensual sexual contact with Jenny after she lied to him about her age. In a case like that the police may arrest Johnny first, take him to the police station, and then tell him: "Jenny accused you of sexual assault. You are being arrested, and this will be referred to the district attorney's office. You could be facing a felony sex-crime charge based on these allegations against you."

The police would do this, of course, knowing full well that it would get Johnny talking, and he'd likely blurt out something incriminating like "It was consensual! I didn't assault her!" However, because the police did not put the information into question form—for example, "Johnny, did you have sex with Jenny last night?"—but instead cloaked their question in the form of a statement, a judge might find that there was technically no interrogation. After all, the prosecutor would argue, the police were merely informing

Johnny of the reason for his arrest, and were not questioning him. Without the interrogation, there is no need for *Miranda*. Confession obtained. Case closed.

■ ■ ■

There are cases, of course, where custodial interrogation happens; that is, the police have no option but to first arrest a person, and *then* ask him or her direct questions. The police don't like this because, under these circumstances, they must (or should) read the person the *Miranda* warnings. But don't worry; all is not lost for the government. After giving the *Miranda* warnings, the police have several methods to induce a suspect to waive, or give up, the right to remain silent and the right to an attorney. The most common method of convincing a suspect to talk is simply to make promises—usually false promises—about how things will be better if he or she does talk, or threaten that things will be worse if he or she doesn't.

Consider this example: You are arrested and read your *Miranda* rights. You're obviously a suspect, and the police want to question you. Whether you've done something illegal—and whether you even *know* that you've done something illegal—doesn't really matter. You're scared to death at this point. You've never been through this before. You've been placed in a physically and emotionally uncomfortable place, away from all familiar surroundings—which was actually done by purposeful and careful design—and you don't know what's going to happen next. What should you do? Should you talk? You've got two cops breathing down your neck in this small, windowless interrogation room, pressuring you. You're thinking about remaining silent, or asking for a lawyer, or both, if that's allowed. Then, the police offer you some persuasive assistance.

Good Cop: In my experience, people who cooperate get treated better by the system.

Bad Cop: All I know is that if he doesn't talk, things are going to be worse for him; and I'm about tired of dickin' around here.

Good Cop: I know the assistant district attorneys, and they take that into account, you know, whether you cooperate. If you're gonna play hardball, they play hardball. But if you're gonna talk, you can really help yourself.

Bad Cop: To hell with him. He don't wanna talk, so let's book him and be done with this. Let the district attorney throw the book at him.

Good Cop: Well, what do you want to do? You've heard Bad Cop. I can only help you so much. This is your opportunity to tell your side of what happened. This is your opportunity to help yourself. What do you want to do? We're not gonna come back here to talk again. This is your only opportunity.

If you're the focus of this common tactic, chances are your fear is growing by the second. At this point you're only thinking about your family and how badly you want to get back to them. You want leniency, and the good cop seems nice and trustworthy. (Later in the day, their roles will be reversed and some other suspect in some other case will be thinking the same thing about your bad cop.) Good Cop has also used the word "opportunity" so many times that you're starting to believe it. Okay, you're persuaded. So you talk. Much like Johnny in chapter 2, you unknowingly admit to committing a crime. Confession obtained. Case closed.

But when a person waives his or her *Miranda* rights, which includes the right to remain silent, doesn't the person have to do so voluntarily? If the police can just bully it out of suspects, or induce them to talk by making false promises, that wouldn't be very fair. If that's the case, what's the point of even requiring the warnings in the first place?

That's a very good argument, but it won't carry the day. Even though you made the statements in response to Good Cop's promise that things would be easier for you if you talked, and Bad Cop's corollary threat that things could get ugly for you if you didn't, it doesn't matter. Why? Because the police avoided making you any *specific* promises. For example, no one told you that "if you talk now, you'll only get charged with a misdemeanor, and there won't be any felony charges." Instead, the police used generalities. They said that if you talked, you could "really help yourself." They left the specifics up to your imagination, which often works better than any promises they could even dream of making.

This simple police strategy—refraining from making any specific promises—allows the court to focus on the technical form of what the police said, rather than the substance of what they were actually doing. This form-over-substance analysis allows a court to decide that, because no specific promise was made, your *Miranda* waiver was voluntary and, more importantly, legally valid. One court, in a published court case, put it this way: "An officer telling a defendant that his cooperation would be to his benefit is not coercive conduct, at least so long as leniency is not promised."[7]

Read that last quote again, and then try to answer this question: If an officer tells an already arrested suspect that cooperating "would be to his benefit," how is that anything *other than* promising "leniency"? What "benefit," other than "leniency," could the arrested suspect possibly anticipate at that point? A three-day trip to an amusement park? A nice dinner and a play?

Of course not. The defendant decided to talk in exchange for the benefit of leniency. Despite this inescapable, commonsense conclusion, however, judges simply torture the plain meaning of ordinary words in order to reach their desired outcome: the destruction of our right to remain silent. As you'll see throughout this book, this type of form-over-substance reasoning consistently produces nonsensical conclusions that wouldn't even earn a passing grade on a first-year law-school exam.[8] But it's the law.

■ ■ ■

We now know that police can skip *Miranda* altogether by simply questioning the suspect before he or she is formally arrested. Or, if they want or need to arrest the suspect first, they can simply avoid a formal interrogation by masking their questions in the form of statements. We also know that when the police must give *Miranda* warnings, they can probably still induce a suspect to waive his or her *Miranda* rights, including the right to an attorney and the right to remain silent.

But what if the police are having a really, really bad day? What if they had to actually arrest the suspect *and* give the suspect *Miranda* warnings *and* he or she refused to talk, despite their best, legally permissible efforts of persuasion? Granted, this is a highly unusual scenario; the majority of suspects who are read their warnings are eventually convinced to waive their rights. (Inexplicably, many people continue to believe that they'll be better off if they confess to a crime.) But sometimes suspects still exercise their right to remain silent. What then?

If that's the case, the police can simply resort to more extreme measures, such as using very specific and clearly impermissible promises and threats, including threats against a suspect's spouse or children. How can they get away with that? Simple: If the suspect refuses to waive his or her rights, and if the police honor the suspect's right to remain silent or the request for an attorney, the police will get no information at all, and therefore the prosecutor will have nothing to use against the suspect in court. Alternatively, if the police push further and ultimately coerce the suspect into waiving his or her *Miranda* rights, the worst-case scenario for the government is that the statement can't be used at trial. (In other words, the case itself doesn't get dismissed because there was a *Miranda* violation.) Therefore, the police are no worse off than if they had honored the suspect's right to remain silent.

However, it gets even better for the government than this no-lose situation would at first suggest; in fact, there is actually a tremendous upside for the government. If the police coerce a *Miranda* waiver and get a statement, the statement may actually lead to the discovery of physical evidence. In that case, while the statement itself could not be used at the defendant's trial, the physical evidence discovered as a result of the statement could be retrieved by the police and, in some cases and in some states, be used at trial.[9] Additionally, the coerced statement could even lead the police to additional suspects, who could then be arrested and prosecuted separately. Therefore, the police are actually far better off having coerced the suspect into waiving his or her rights than if they had honored the suspect's right to remain silent. This, of course, provides the perverse incentive for the police to violate, rather than respect, our constitutional right against self-incrimination.

Additionally, the inadmissible statement itself, even though obtained in violation of *Miranda*, will not be excluded from the defendant's trial in all situations. While the prosecutor might not be allowed to use the defendant's statement in the first portion of the criminal trial—the portion known as the prosecutor's case-in-chief—he or she could still use it in trial as impeachment evidence.[10] What this means is that, should the defendant choose to testify at trial in his or her own defense, and should the defendant testify even the slightest bit differently from the earlier statement obtained in violation of *Miranda* (or, more accurately, the interrogator's *version* of that statement), the statement would then become admissible at trial to contradict or impeach the defendant's trial testimony. This may strongly deter the defendant from testifying and, worse yet, may lead the jury to believe that the defendant is not testifying because he or she is guilty and has something to hide.

■ ■ ■

You can see by now that, unlike the sexual assault of a child law that was discussed in chapter 2, the right to remain silent is incredibly malleable and easily manipulated. What was intended to be an absolute right against self-incrimination has morphed into a free pass—in fact, an incentive—for the police to use whatever means possible to force a *Miranda* waiver and violate our right against self-incrimination. But it gets even better than that, if you can believe it.

Let's suppose that the prosecutor really wants to use the defendant's statement at trial in the case-in-chief; using it as impeachment evidence just isn't good enough because there's a chance that the defendant may choose not to testify, in which case there would be nothing to impeach. Without the statement as part of the case-in-chief, the government's case would take a huge hit. The problem for the prosecutor, however, is that before the police were able to get the statement, the defendant first requested a lawyer. This request was repeatedly ignored by the police, meaning that the statement was obtained in violation of *Miranda*, and is not admissible in the prosecutor's case-in-chief. What happens then?

In that case, the judge can come to the rescue of the police and prosecutor and resort to the old standby described earlier: the form-over-substance analysis. The court can simply rule, from high on the judicial throne, that the defendant's request for a lawyer really wasn't a "request for a lawyer" after all. Rather, it was ambiguous, and no reasonably intelligent police officer could have interpreted the defendant's words to mean that the defendant wanted a lawyer. For example, consider this exchange, which includes actual language from published court cases:

Officer: I've read you your rights. Now, sign here where it says, "I hereby waive these rights," so you can take this opportunity to talk to me.

Suspect: Maybe I should talk to a lawyer.

Officer: What do you mean, maybe you should talk to a lawyer? This is your one opportunity. I'm not coming back here again. If you want to help yourself, you have to do it now.

Suspect: I can't afford a lawyer. Is there any way I can get one?

Officer: Why don't we talk about what you were doing last night?

Suspect: Could I get a lawyer?

Officer: What were you doing last night?

Suspect: All right, all right . . .

The courts can, and have, tortured the plain meaning of these words and simply concluded that the suspect did not make an "unequivocal request" for a lawyer.[11] Consequently, because the *Miranda* right was not, in the court's view, properly invoked by the suspect, there was no *Miranda* violation, and the statement can be used by the prosecutor at trial, even in the case-in-chief. How can the courts do this? Well, they have simply ruled, presumably with straight faces, that a reasonably intelligent police officer, hearing the above language, could only conclude that the suspect *might* be requesting a lawyer. Even the language "could I get a lawyer?" is simply not enough to invoke the right to counsel. Further, the courts go on, tongue in cheek, to concede that it would have been the better practice for the police officer to clarify what the suspect meant by the request; however, it was not the officer's duty to do so, and therefore *Miranda* rights were never properly invoked.[12] (No doubt the officer was eager to adopt the court's best-practices suggestion for future interrogations.)

To illustrate how insulting this legal holding really is, consider the above exchange in a different context. Suppose you pumped some gas for your car and then went into the gas station to pay for it. While inside, you wanted to take your chance on the weekly lottery, so you attempted to buy a lottery ticket. If the cashier were as mentally dim as the police pretended to be in the *Miranda* context, you would never be able to successfully buy the lottery ticket. Your verbal exchange with the cashier might go something like this:

Cashier: Do you want to pay for that gas?

You: Yeah, and hey, maybe I'll take one of those lottery tickets, too.

Cashier: Okay, that's forty dollars for the gas.

You: Here's forty-one dollars; can I get a lottery ticket for tonight's drawing?

Cashier: Just gas? Great.

You: Could I get one of those lottery tickets?

Cashier: That's a good quality of petrol we sell, you know? So, nothing other than the gas, then?

You: Whatever! Forget the ticket; I'll buy it down the street.

When you take the identical language and put it in another context such as this, you can see just how ridiculous these court rulings are. Is there anything unclear about "can I get a lottery ticket?" Of course not. It's a request for a lottery ticket. Likewise, when a suspect asks "can I get a lawyer?" he or she is requesting a lawyer. Also remember that the suspect is arrested and can't go anywhere. How else is the suspect supposed to get this faceless, nameless lawyer that the cop just offered? There's nothing ambiguous about this request, nor is there anything for the officer to clarify, and we all know that. Nonetheless, judges can once again use their now familiar form-over-substance analysis—by being hypercritical of the form of the suspect's request instead of focusing on the substance of what the suspect is requesting—to justify their destruction of our constitutional right against self-incrimination.

■ ■ ■

Why is all of this important? Who cares if a guilty person confesses? Well, we covered constitutional rights and the factually guilty in the context of our marijuana-cigarette example from chapter 2, and we know that if the Constitution is to protect anyone, it must protect everyone. In addition, however, there are other very specific dangers when the right to remain silent or the right to an attorney is not honored. As we showed in Johnny's sexual assault of a child example in chapter 2, the suspect could be a person who has done absolutely nothing morally or ethically wrong, and in fact could be the true victim. In that case, the rights enumerated in *Miranda* could save the suspect from the life-ruining intentions of the government.

Similarly, this could well be a case where the suspect *has* done something wrong, but the "confession" will be used in the prosecution of a much more serious, and unsubstantiated, criminal allegation. Remember, there are hundreds upon hundreds, if not a thousand or more, different crimes in each state. The prosecutor won't want to settle for charging a misdemeanor if he or she can squeeze out a felony. Nor will the prosecutor be happy charging a lower felony when charging a more serious felony can be justified. The greater the number and severity of the charges, the more likely the prosecutor can pressure the defendant to waive the right to trial and accept a plea deal, which results in more convictions with less effort. (Yes, legalized extortion happens not only during police interrogations, but throughout the criminal process.)

Finally, trampling the right to remain silent poses an additional risk—the risk of a false confession. In this chapter we have examined some of the techniques that police use to either circumvent or overcome *Miranda*. But remember, this all occurs *pre*interrogation. Only once the actual interrogation commences does the real fun begin. Interrogations can last hours or days and are, by specific design, highly uncomfortable, both physically and emotionally. Further, they begin with the police officers' presumption of guilt and often don't end until the suspect has adopted a story, forced on him or her by police, that is consistent with the police officers' beliefs about what happened. Along the way, the police will employ a variety of physical and psychological tactics—including the fabrication of physical evidence or eyewitnesses—to overcome any resistance. Should the police grow tired, a new team of interrogators can be brought in to take over the show. The process is designed so that the suspect sees no viable alternative other than to agree with the police, regardless of whether their version of events turns out to be factually accurate.

These well-honed, highly aggressive techniques do, no doubt, lead to some factually true confessions. However, the problem is that they also lead to some false confessions, which in turn lead to wrongful convictions. False-confession and wrongful-conviction cases—which actually occur far more frequently than most people think—have been well documented and studied by research psychologists. Thanks to recent laws requiring that some interrogations be videotaped, and to funding for postconviction DNA testing, some of our wrongfully convicted citizens have now been exonerated—many after decades in prison. This includes, for example, the young boys who were forced to falsely confess in the infamous Central Park jogger case. [13]

The continued risk of false confessions, however, is quite real. In fact, the risk is particularly high for the weakest among us: juveniles; those with limited mental capacity; those who are mentally ill; and those who are intoxicated or physically ill at the time of their interrogation. False confessions, of course, would not occur—or at least would occur far less frequently—if suspects' *Miranda* invocations were scrupulously honored rather than ignored or trampled.

■ ■ ■

We have now seen, in the context of the right against self-incrimination, how a soft, malleable right can be easily sidestepped by police. Further, in the rare cases where the police are unable to accomplish their goal, the right can simply be destroyed by prosecutors and judges in the courtroom. We will see these scenarios repeat themselves, with slight variations, as we explore the treatment of other constitutional rights throughout the criminal process.

NOTES

1. "No person . . . shall be compelled in any criminal case to be a witness against himself . . ." United States Constitution, Fifth Amendment, at topics.law.cornell.edu/constitution/fifth_amendment (accessed March 26, 2010).

2. *Miranda v. Arizona*, 384 U.S. 436 (1966).

3. For an entertaining discussion of the mess that courts have made out of what should be a simple *Miranda* warning, see Michael D. Cicchini, "The New Miranda Warning," Marquette University Law School Faculty Blog, November 8, 2010, at law.marquette.edu/facultyblog/2010/11/08/the-new-miranda-warning/ (accessed March 12, 2011).

4. See *U.S. v. Yusuff*, 96 F.3d 982 (7th Cir. 1996).

5. *Yarborough v. Alvarado*, 541 U.S. 652 (2004).

6. See *Enoch v. Gramley*, 70 F.3d 1490 (7th Cir. 1995).

7. *State v. Deets*, 523 N.W.2d 180 (Wis. Ct. App. 1994). This issue also arises in the context of determining whether the statement itself, in addition to the waiver of *Miranda* rights, is voluntary.

8. For more examples of this tortured reasoning in the *Miranda* context, see Michael D. Cicchini, "The New Miranda Warning."

9. For cases discussing the use of physical evidence obtained from a *Miranda* violation, see *U.S. v. Gravens*, 129 F.3d 974 (7th Cir. 1997), and *State v. Knapp*, 2005 WI 27.

10. See *Harris v. New York*, 401 U.S. 222 (1971), and *Ameen v. State*, 186 N.W.2d 206 (Wis. 1971).

11. See *Davis v. U.S.*, 512 U.S. 452 (1994; "Maybe I should talk to a lawyer" not sufficient to invoke *Miranda* right); *Lord v. Duckworth*, 29 F.3d 1216 (7th Cir. 1994; "I can't afford a lawyer, but is there any way I can get one?" not sufficient to invoke *Miranda* right); and *U.S. v. Wesela*, 223 F.3d 656 (7th Cir. 2000; "Could I get a lawyer?" not sufficient to invoke *Miranda* right). See also Michael D. Cicchini, "The New Miranda Warning."

12. See *Davis v. U.S.*; *Lord v. Duckworth*; and *U.S. v. Wesela*.

13. For an article on interrogation tactics, false confessions, and wrongful convictions that includes hundreds of footnotes to relevant studies, articles, and cases (including an article about the Central Park jogger case), see Daniel E. Chojnacki, Michael D. Cicchini, and Lawrence T. White, "An Empirical Basis for the Admission of Expert Testimony on False Confessions," 40 *Arizona State Law Journal* 1 (2008), available at cicchinilaw.com/PDFs/Cicchini_Final_050608.pdf (accessed March 12, 2011).

Chapter Five

Privacy

You Have the Right to Be Secure in Your Home (Unless We Really Want to Come In)

The saying "A man's home is his castle" has been with us for centuries.[1] Despite the passage of time, however, it means as much today as when it was first uttered. In fact, today it has meaning not only for a handful of white, male landowners, but for all of us. No matter our sex, race, social status, or income level, our home is our castle and no one, especially not the government or its agents, should be allowed to enter it and violate our privacy.

Sounds good, right? Well, it's far from true. Although the Constitution still, in theory, ensures our right to be secure in our homes and free from government intrusion, the right of privacy is, once again, a soft law. As we learned in chapter 4, that means that it's only as strong as the government agents—the police, prosecutors, and judges—say it is. Sure, the U.S. Supreme Court still says that "physical entry of the home is the *chief evil* against which the wording of the [Constitution] is directed."[2] But, as we'll soon see, talk is cheap.

■ ■ ■

As with any constitutional right, we have to start with a general rule: "The right of the people to be secure in their persons, houses, papers, and effects, against unreasonable searches and seizures, shall not be violated . . ."[3] But what constitutes an unreasonable search? For starters, a government search of a citizen's home is presumed, by law, to be unreasonable—that is, illegal—unless the police have a search warrant. [4]

A search warrant—or, more simply, a warrant—is a document ordering the police to search a home. [5] It essentially works like this: The police learn of allegations or obtain other evidence that a suspect's home may contain contraband, or physical evidence of a crime. (Maybe the contraband is a marijuana cigarette, as we saw in chapter 2, or maybe it's something completely different, like a firearm or a computer hard drive.) Then, based on these allegations or other evidence, the police put together a written statement of facts and beliefs, and must swear to them under oath. [6] (Because this is done in secret, no one ever gets to see the police officer swear under oath; therefore, we can only take the word of the police that this happens.) This sworn, written statement describes what the police saw, heard, know, or believe with regard to the alleged criminal activity. It must also indicate why they believe that the specific home being targeted contains evidence of the crime.

The police then take this sworn, written statement to a judge or court commissioner—that is, a neutral and detached magistrate—who will, in theory, review it. The magistrate then decides whether the sworn, written statement is legally sufficient to support the issuance of a warrant. The statement will only be legally sufficient if the source of the information is reliable, and if the information is detailed enough to establish "probable cause" to believe that the targeted home contains contraband. [7] If the police meet this standard, the magistrate will then sign a warrant that permits—in fact, orders—the police to search the home. The warrant itself must also be very particular in its description of which home the police are ordered to search, where the home is located, and why the police want, and are now ordered, to search it.

On its face, this warrant requirement would seem to offer us substantial protection from government intrusion into our homes. As is usually the case, however, the devil is in the details. As you might have guessed, the strength of this constitutional right of privacy depends not only on how broadly the courts actually define a valid warrant, but also on the myriad of exceptions that have been created to get around the warrant requirement altogether.

■ ■ ■

Let's start with a simple example. Suppose you're at home one day and a neighbor comes by, looking to sell you some marijuana. He doesn't come to you out of the blue; he knows you and has been to your house a couple of times. The two of you also smoked marijuana together at a party last year.

However, you have no interest in buying any marijuana. You rarely smoke it; in fact, the last time you had any was nearly one full year ago at that party. And you certainly don't want any in your house, as you have a daughter who lives with you a good deal of the time. In a nice way, you send this guy packing and think nothing of it.

Later that night, however, the police are at your door, and they've got a warrant. They enter your home, pat you down, handcuff you, and then search your home while you watch helplessly. They rifle through all of your rooms, your closets, your clothing, your documents, and your other possessions—including the mundane, the private, and the embarrassing. (You're lucky your daughter is with your ex-spouse that day, so you've avoided being completely humiliated in front of her.)

You don't know what the police are doing at your house, or what they're looking for. You wonder if this is just a mistake, or if someone has falsely accused you of a crime. As your mind races you start to panic, but you finally muster the strength to ask the police what's going on. They scream at you to "shut up" and briskly go about their business, as if they're searching for high-level terrorists that are hiding out in your home. You sit there handcuffed, helpless, scared, and confused.

This fiasco finally ends with the police holding a pill bottle that they found in your bathroom. You're led off in handcuffs, out of your home, to the county jail. When you arrive downtown, the police finally tell you what this is all about: your neighbor was arrested for possession of marijuana, and he said he got it *from you*. And that pill bottle—the one they found when searching your house for the marijuana supply that doesn't exist—had someone else's name on it. The police inform you that you'll probably be charged with felony *delivery* of marijuana—based solely on your neighbor's accusation and despite the complete lack of physical evidence—and misdemeanor theft of prescription drugs.

You can't believe this is happening. You know—or at least *think*—that you've done nothing wrong, so you are eager to clear up this misunderstanding. You waive your *Miranda* rights because you just want to tell the police the truth so you can get home and fix the damage they caused to your otherwise orderly existence. You voluntarily explain that your neighbor came to *your* house to try to sell *you* the marijuana, and you turned him away. Sure, you knew him, and you even admit, when questioned by police, that he'd been to your house before and that you saw him at that party last year. But you never gave him any drugs; *he's* the drug dealer. As for the prescription bottle with someone else's name on it, you didn't steal that, you explain. It belongs to your ex-spouse, and your ex-spouse *gave* it to you. Further, it only had three prescription sleeping pills in it, and you hadn't even taken one yet. You were having trouble sleeping, and your ex-spouse suggested that you try those pills. If you ended up liking them, you were going to ask your doctor for a prescription.

Contrary to your plan, however, you don't get to go home that night; instead, you'll be a guest at the county jail for the evening. To make matters worse, all of your statements, including the seemingly innocent one about your past relationship with your pot-toting neighbor, find their way into your criminal complaint to support the two allegations against you. First, you are charged with delivery of marijuana to your neighbor. (Your neighbor, however, is only charged with simple possession, a misdemeanor, because he lied about you to take the heat off himself. The police don't care; they now get two defendants for the price of one.) Your statements to police that you knew this guy, that he'd been to your house before, and that you'd partied together in the past are all taken out of context. Now selectively incorporated into the criminal complaint, these statements are transformed into quasi confessions and magically support, rather than refute, the accusation that *you* delivered marijuana to your neighbor. It's amazing how important context can be.

Second, you're also charged with illegal possession (no longer theft) of a controlled substance without a prescription. It turns out that although your statement about the sleeping pills exonerated you of theft, you actually admitted to a different crime in the process. Interestingly, the police tell you that your statement also got your ex-spouse, who gave you the sleeping pills, charged with *delivery* of a controlled substance. This will be great for your daughter, who might soon have two convicts as parents.

In any case, as you sit in jail staring at a copy of your freshly drafted criminal complaint, you simply can't believe the situation you're in. While you're no angel, you've always considered yourself to be a fairly law-abiding citizen. And you're definitely a good person, unlike the people that they show on *Cops* and the police television dramas. And as you sit and think, you also start to convince yourself that murderers and sex offenders routinely go unpunished by the system, yet *you* are somehow being unjustly targeted for your extremely minor transgression.

So after you are released (at least temporarily) from custody, you decide to get a lawyer and fight your case. As you sit in your lawyer's office for your first meeting, he mentions that your constitutional rights might have been violated; that is, the search of your home might have been illegal because the warrant may have been invalid. He also tells you that any evidence, including the pill bottle and possibly even your statements, might be suppressed.

However, your lawyer also explains that this will be a long shot. First, there is a legal presumption that the warrant is valid, as long as it was signed by a neutral and detached magistrate. Second, there is a presumption that any judge or commissioner, by virtue of *being* a judge or commissioner, is a neutral and detached magistrate.[8] When something is presumed by law, that means it is assumed to be true, and the burden then shifts to the other side—here, you and your lawyer—to disprove it. In criminal law, these presumptions are legal fictions that are usually created for the benefit of the government.

Despite this presumption of neutrality, your lawyer explains that, in reality, getting a judge to sign a search warrant is a mere formality for the police. In nearly every instance, it's an automatic rubber stamp. Only in the rarest of cases has a request for a search warrant been turned down. In fact, your lawyer explains that instead of being neutral, the particular judge that signed your search warrant probably did so without even reading the sworn statement or the warrant. The big tip-off, your lawyer says, is that the address and other descriptions in the sworn statement requesting the warrant are completely different from the address and other descriptions in the warrant itself—an elephant-size cut-and-paste error that would have been caught by anyone who bothered to read the documents.

But your lawyer also suspects that the judge didn't even read the documents based on his experience with this judge in the past. That is, some of the criminal complaints that this judge has signed off on in other cases were actually later dismissed, by the *same judge*, once your lawyer got the chance to argue in court that the complaints were incredibly defective and completely devoid of probable cause. If the judge had actually read those complaints *before* signing them, as he was supposed to have done, he would have realized their defects and never would have signed them in the first place. So your lawyer suspects that the judge's rubber-stamp approach to criminal complaints probably carries over to search warrants. Yet the law presumes this judge to be neutral and detached, which in turn leads to the presumption that the warrant is valid. You now start to get an idea of what you're up against when challenging this warrant.

Aside from whether the judge even read the documents—something you'll never be able to disprove anyway—your lawyer tells you that the warrant and other documents in your case are, in fact, particularly shoddy. For example, the warrant doesn't really accurately describe your home, and doesn't state in any level of detail what the police are to seize once they get inside of your home. On top of that, the sworn statement in support of the warrant has its own set of problems, including its reliance on the hearsay statement of your pot-toting neighbor—a man who was in hot water and looking to save his own backside when he made up the accusation against you.

Despite these defects, your lawyer cautions, the test for whether a warrant is valid is quite liberal.[9] Nonetheless, he decides to challenge the legality of the warrant and files a motion to suppress evidence in front of the judge in your criminal case. If this judge finds that the warrant issued by the first judge—a colleague whom he sees on a daily basis and with whom he is likely friends—is legally defective, then you win. All of the evidence against you *might* then be suppressed (more on that later), which means that the state's case will either go away or, at the very least, be much weaker.

When you finally get to court for the judge's long-awaited decision, however, not only do you lose your motion to suppress the evidence, but your judge isn't at all happy about your lawyer trying to use this "technicality" on your behalf. In fact, he doesn't just rule against you; he also decides to take advantage of a captive audience (you and your lawyer) to lecture about it. Additionally, because your lawyer had the nerve to point out the shoddy work of the police and the judiciary, yelling is also appropriate. And in the end, even though the judge has to concede that the warrant was defective in several ways, he nonetheless denies your motion to suppress the evidence based on something called the good-faith exception. [10]

The good-faith exception is one of the more dangerous exceptions to the Constitution. Here's how it works: First, the judge who signed the warrant was presumed to be neutral and detached, so the warrant itself was presumed valid. However, you later overcame this presumption by proving that the warrant was, in fact, legally defective. So you win, right? Not so fast. Under the good-faith exception, if the police officers who applied for and obtained the warrant acted in good faith, the search of your home will be deemed legal, despite the defective warrant. How, you ask, can the officers prove that they acted in good faith? As you might have guessed, it's quite easy, and it involves another one of those presumptions. An officer is presumed to have acted in good faith by the mere fact that he or she went to the judge to apply for the warrant in the first place.

But don't worry. The law gives you the opportunity to rebut this presumption of good faith. All you have to do is prove that the police officer—who never went to law school and is not licensed to practice law—should have known that the warrant was legally defective, even though the educated, neutral, and detached judge declared that it was legally valid by signing it. Good luck with that.

The end result is that, under the good-faith exception, the very act of getting a warrant usually makes the warrant itself valid, no matter how defective the warrant actually is. Yes, it really is that easy, and that circular. This exception, of course, swallows the rule whole. In other words, the general rule—that the police have to have a valid warrant to search your home—is decimated by the exception to that rule.

■ ■ ■

It is clear that the good-faith exception validates most police searches made pursuant to most warrants, no matter how defective a warrant may be. But what if the police don't want to get a warrant? Don't worry. The law gives the police numerous ways to get around the warrant requirement entirely.

These ways around, or exceptions to, the warrant requirement include the special-needs exception, the consent to search exception, the third-party consent to search exception, the search incident to arrest in the home exception, the protective-sweep exception, the abandonment rule, the plain-view doctrine, and the emergency (exigent circumstances) exception—including its many variations, such as hot pursuit, the destruction of evidence, and community safety. And there are others, as well.

Based solely on the sheer number of exceptions, you're probably thinking that the warrant requirement really isn't a requirement after all. And you'd be right to think this. It would be more accurate to call it a suggestion rather than a requirement. And while we certainly won't address all of the exceptions to the warrant requirement, a few of them merit special attention. Let's start with the consent to search exception, which is probably the most common way for the police to elude the warrant requirement altogether.

The consent to search exception is simple. If you allow the police to enter and search your home, they can do so based solely on that consent, and without a warrant.[11] Who in their right minds would give police consent to even enter their homes, let alone search them? Well, actually, most people don't—at least not at first. It is true that with some constitutional rights, people will often waive them because they think it will be in their best interest to do so. For example, with regard to the right to remain silent and the right to an attorney, suspects may think—and not unreasonably so, based on the unclear language of the *Miranda* warning—that if they request a lawyer it would either look bad or be used against them in court. Or they may think that their cooperation will help them in the long run. Or they may think that they have done nothing wrong and simply want to clear the whole thing up.

Some of these factors may also be relevant when a person decides whether to give the police permission to search a home. However, chances are that if a person has something illegal in the home, the person would usually know it, and would probably not give police the consent they're asking for. Why, then, do so many people give consent? The answer lies in this riddle: What's the difference between a vampire and a cop? Answer: A vampire has to actually be invited in before entering your home, but a cop just has to *say* that you invited him in. In other words, the police officer can outright lie and say that you gave consent by your words or even by your actions, as interpreted by the officer. Or, more commonly, the officer can simply coerce you into consenting—a strategy yet to be successfully employed by any vampire in any Hollywood movie.

An example will better illustrate this consent to search exception. Suppose the police come to your house, without a warrant, and ask to search your home for evidence of a crime they are investigating. You wisely say, "No, absolutely not." What do you think they're going to do next—give up and go for a cup of coffee? Possible, but unlikely. We already know how unwilling the police are to accept the invocation of our constitutional rights—remember the request for a lawyer in chapter 4? And much like getting around your right to remain silent, the police have several weapons in their arsenal to get around your right of privacy.

Interestingly, however, unlike *Miranda* and the right to remain silent, the police do not have to inform you that you have the right to refuse to give consent to search your home. Therefore, even if you say no at first, the police can simply keep asking you, each time in a more persuasive manner than the time before, until you acquiesce.[12] If that doesn't work, they can simply tell you that if you don't consent to a search, they'll just have to go through the trouble of arresting you, getting a warrant, and searching without your being there. (Of course, in order to uphold the legality of this tactic, the officer may have to later testify that this threat was genuine rather than a mere pretext, but this testimony would, of course, be very difficult to disprove.)[13] And if you're not swayed by any of those tactics, the police can simply create a more intimidating setting by first arresting you and taking you to a specially designed interrogation room, and then going back to other tactics. This is known simply as the arrest and repeat approach.[14]

If the police are just striking out all over the place in their goal of searching your home without a warrant, don't worry for them. Chances are they still won't have to go through the trouble of applying for that warrant. They still have other strategies available, including the one used in the following exchange.[15]

Officer: We want to search your home.

Citizen: No. You can't come in. Get a warrant if you can; otherwise, leave me alone.

Officer: It would be a shame if we had to go get a warrant and come back here to find whatever it is that we might find. I know you've got family members. It would be a shame if we happened to find something illegal in areas of the house where they have access, like the living room or family room. Who knows where we might find something? Who knows if the prosecutor would charge them, too?

Citizen: I said get a warrant!

Officer: I'm just sayin'. I mean, you don't want to bring all of them down with you, do you? Your wife and your daughter . . . they got nothin' to do with this, right? What kind of man does that? Why don't you just let us in right now? It'll be easier on everyone. Let us just look around, see if we find what we want to find, and nothing will get pinned on them.

Citizen: All right.

Is this legal? Remember, much like the case of waiving the *Miranda* rights, giving consent to search has to be voluntary, not coerced. No matter. The type of threat described above has been held to be perfectly legal; that is, the suspect's consent to search under those circumstances was *still* held to be voluntary. In the real-life case like the one above, the court simply decided that the citizen was concerned, not because of the officer's threat to his family members, but because he had something illegal in his house. (A closer analysis, of course, reveals that before the threat was made to his family, the citizen didn't seem at all "concerned" and flatly refused to give consent to enter his home.)

Here, once again, it becomes painfully evident that yet another of our constitutional rights is a soft law. The right of privacy is mere putty in the hands of police, and later of prosecutors and judges in the courtroom, if the defendant decides to actually challenge the legality of the search. The judge can rely on any factor that he or she wishes when deciding that the consent was voluntary. This analysis is called a facts-and-circumstances test—a test we'll discuss in more detail in chapter 6. It essentially means that the judge can look at any counterbalancing fact or circumstance—for example, that the defendant was experienced in dealing with police, that the defendant was educated, or that the defendant was *not* intoxicated at the time of supposedly giving consent—to support a decision that the consent was voluntarily given. The judge will look at the totality of the circumstances and attach any weight he or she wishes to any particular fact or circumstance he or she chooses.[16] This allows the judge to decide that, although the police acted in a *coercive manner*, the consent itself was *not coerced*. A subtle distinction, and one in which a crafty judge will, no doubt, take great pride.

There are many other exceptions to the warrant requirement. The more commonly used exceptions include the emergency, or exigent circumstances exception; that is, the police *had* to enter right then and there without a warrant because they thought, for example, that someone inside could be in danger.[17] When the defendant later challenges the legality of this warrantless entry and search, it's quite easy for the police and prosecutor to defeat the defendant's challenge. After all, virtually any noise of any kind emanating from inside the home will support the possibility that there was a potential danger. It doesn't matter that, in fact, there was no danger whatsoever. The important thing is that the police now say they thought that there could have been danger at the time they decided to enter.

Another commonly used exception to enter a home without a warrant is the protective-sweep exception.[18] Suppose you allow the police into your living room, at their request, to discuss a matter. Once you invite them into any part of your home, they may be allowed to look around other parts of your home—the so-called protective sweep—to check for other people and make sure there isn't a risk to police safety. The police might even use this exception to justify their search of very small areas—for example, the pocket of your jacket hanging in your closet—even though a person could never fit in those areas.

In this area of constitutional law, the examples are limitless. The facts-and-circumstances nature of the analysis ensures not only endless variety, but also unlimited entertainment—unless, of course, you are the defendant whose rights were violated. Furthermore, the exceptions discussed above are only a few of the ones that can be used to justify a warrantless entry of the home. The contents of the court decisions are constrained only by police audacity, prosecutorial creativity, and judicial boldness.

But in the event that the courts have failed to cover every imaginable base, they've developed yet another exception, which is known as the inevitable-discovery rule.[19] This rule can be used to uphold any warrant*less* search, much like the good-faith exception upholds any warrant-*based* search. For the police, the inevitable-discovery rule is the safety net of all safety nets, and the catch-all of all catch-alls. Even if the police do everything wrong, and the prosecutor simply is unable to formulate any viable argument in support of the search, and the judge seems to be left with no choice but to find that the warrantless search was illegal, the inevitable-discovery rule could still validate the search.

Consider this example: Suppose that the police want to search your home without a warrant. They could, if they wanted, simply apply for and obtain a warrant. Then, it would be legal to search your home even if the warrant turned out to be defective, thanks to the good-faith exception discussed earlier. But they don't want to do that. Instead, they decide to get verbal consent to search your home from a third party—for example, your spouse—which is much easier than getting a warrant. During the search they find evidence against you that the prosecutor will want to use at your future criminal trial.

When your case finally gets to court, however, your lawyer points out that the police were actually mistaken. The person that consented to the search of your home really wasn't your spouse, and in fact didn't even live there. The police didn't care about these details at that time; rather, they were just looking for quick and easy access. They didn't bother to ask the person's identity, or whether this person had the authority to let the police into your home. The police really botched this one. And this is precisely the type of situation where the inevitable-discovery rule will save the day.

The inevitable-discovery rule states that even if the police illegally entered and searched your home without a warrant, and even if none of the exceptions to the warrant requirement apply, all the police have to do is say that had they not searched illegally, they would have applied for a warrant or somehow would have obtained the evidence by legal means. Therefore, the evidence inevitably would have been discovered anyway.[20] Consequently, the judge will find that there is no harm to you from the warrantless, illegal entry and search of your home. All the police had to do was describe to the judge a possible chain of sequential events that might have happened and might have led to the lawful discovery of the same evidence that they illegally discovered. And they only have to "prove" this hypothetical, contrapositive scenario by a preponderance of the evidence, which, unlike the "beyond a reasonable doubt" standard or the "clear and convincing evidence" standard, is a very low burden of proof.

The inevitable-discovery rule is an even more outrageous bailout scheme than the good-faith exception. At least under the good-faith exception, the police had to actually go through the process of getting the warrant, no matter how legally defective the warrant turned out to be. But with the inevitable-discovery rule, all the police have to do is say that they *would have* obtained the evidence by legal means, had they not first entered and searched illegally. That's like a teacher allowing a student to avoid punishment for cheating because the student convinces the teacher that he or she would have earned the A even without cheating. If only we could all live in such a world.

■ ■ ■

Despite the loose requirements for what constitutes a valid warrant, and despite the numerous and expansive exceptions to the warrant requirement itself, I've saved the granddaddy of them all for last. Imagine a situation where the police searched your home and did not have a warrant, and the prosecutor could not fit their behavior into one of the numerous exceptions to the warrant requirement. Further imagine that the prosecutor conceded this fact, and neither the prosecutor nor the police could dream up a fake scenario where, had the police not acted illegally, the evidence would have been inevitably discovered by legal means. Finally, imagine that the judge had no way of bailing out the police or the prosecutor. Your rights were violated, and everyone admits it. Period.

So what happens next? The illegally obtained evidence would now be suppressed, or excluded from your trial, right? Probably not. The U.S. Supreme Court has held that, while a citizen has the right of privacy, no citizen has the right to have illegally obtained evidence suppressed. In fact, the Court has held that when there is a violation of the right of privacy, exclusion of the illegally obtained evidence from the defendant's trial should be "our last resort, not our first impulse."[21]

So when privacy rights are violated, what is the remedy? The Supreme Court's lingo about "last resorts" and "first impulses" is just an annoyingly pretentious way of saying that this whole warrant requirement is much ado about nothing. That is, privacy is a right without a remedy. This leads to the obvious question: What good is our right of privacy if the police can violate it without consequence?[22]

Sometimes just asking the question is enough to provide the obvious answer.

■ ■ ■

As you can see, enforcing constitutional rights is an uphill struggle and usually a losing battle. And this fight doesn't end once you get past suppression motions and start preparing for trial. There are still other constitutional rights to be ignored, circumvented, and flat-out destroyed. In the next chapter, we'll see how the battle continues as we get closer to trial.

NOTES

1. For a history of the phrase "a man's home is his castle," see the Phrase Finder, at www.phrases.org.uk/bulletin_board/8/messages/1239.html (accessed November 1, 2011).

2. *Welsh v. Wisconsin*, 466 U.S. 740 (1984).

3. United States Constitution, Fourth Amendment, at www.law.cornell.edu/constitution/fourth_amendment (accessed November 1, 2011).

4. See *Schneckloth v. Bustamonte*, 412 U.S. 218 (1973).

5. For a discussion of search warrants generally, see *U.S. v. Buckley*, 4 F.3d 552 (7th Cir. 1993).

6. See *State v. Tye*, 2001 WI 24.

7. See *State v. DeSmidt*, 454 N.W.2d 780, 785 (Wis. 1990).

8. See *State v. McBride*, 523 N.W.2d 106 (Wis. Ct. App. 1994).

9. For cases discussing the legality of search warrants, see *U.S. v. Griffin*, 827 F.2d 1108 (7th Cir. 1987; even highly suspect warrants will be deemed valid); *U.S. v. Pless*, 982 F.2d 1118 (7th Cir. 1992; hearsay is acceptable in a warrant); and *U.S. v. Lloyd*, 71 F.3d 1256 (7th Cir. 1995; detailed statement more likely to be reliable).

10. See *U.S. v. Merritt*, 361 F.3d 1005 (7th Cir. 2004).

11. See *State v. Johnston*, 518 N.W.2d 759 (Wis. 1994).

12. See *U.S. v. LaGrone*, 43 F.3d 332 (7th Cir. 1994).

13. See *U.S. v. Evans*, 27 F.3d 1219 (7th Cir. 1994).

14. See *U.S. v. Bernitt*, 392 F.3d 873 (7th Cir. 2004).

15. The hypothetical scenario is based on *U.S. v. Santiago*, 428 F.3d 699 (7th Cir. 2005).

16. See *U.S. v. Raibley*, 243 F.3d 1069 (7th Cir. 2001).

17. See *State v. Boggess*, 340 N.W.2d 516 (Wis. 1983).

18. See *U.S. v. James*, 40 F.3d 850 (7th Cir. 1994).

19. See *Nix v. Williams*, 467 U.S. 431 (1984).

20. See *U.S. v. Brown*, 64 F.3d 1083 (7th Cir. 1995).

21. *Herring v. United States*, 129 S. Ct. 695, 700 (2009; quoting *Hudson v. Michigan*, 547 U.S. 586, 591, 2006).

22. See Michael D. Cicchini, "An Economics Perspective on the Exclusionary Rule and Deterrence" 75 *Missouri Law Review* 459 (2010), at cicchinilaw.com/PDFs/Cicchini_Final_050608.pdf (accessed November 1, 2011).

Chapter Six

Confrontation

You (Might) Have the Right to Cross-examine Your Accuser

The right of confrontation, or the right to cross-examine the state's witnesses against you at trial, is probably the constitutional right that is least likely to be thought of as a mere "technicality" or loophole.[1] After all, talk is cheap, right? Anyone can make an accusation about anything. Most of us appreciate, therefore, that cross-examination serves a legitimate purpose in the criminal justice system. But despite this, the right of confrontation often suffers from a different but equally harmful image in our popular culture.

How many times have we seen on television the poor child victim, or the insulting stereotype of the weak female victim, being badgered by the menacing defense lawyer in court? The defense lawyer, in a loud and thundering voice that solidifies his evil nature, somehow manages to make the witness crumble, thereby allowing the guilty defendant to go free. With the child victim, he may expose the time the child stole a cookie from the cookie jar, thereby destroying the victim's credibility with the jury and, of course, scarring him for life in the process. With the female victim, he may explore her prior sexual encounters for the jury, thereby arguing that she actually invited the crime that was perpetrated upon her. All of this happens while the meek, overmatched prosecutor quietly hangs his head.

Of course, nothing could be further from reality. First, such cross-examination would never happen. With regard to the child witness, any defense lawyer who yells at a child does so at the client's peril, rather than to the client's benefit, and would be shut down rather quickly by the prosecutor and judge. And with regard to the insulting, stereotypically weak female witness, today's "rape shield laws" would, except in the rarest of circumstances, prevent a defendant from telling the jury anything about the witness's prior sexual relationships. [2]

Second, the use of cross-examination at trial, while incredibly valuable, is far less dramatic than anything you'll see on television. Consider a simple example, subtle variations of which fill our courtrooms across this country on a daily basis. Assume that you are falsely accused of burglarizing your next-door neighbor's garage. You are alleged to have broken in at night without consent, and with the intent to damage his car. Your next-door neighbor wasn't home at the time, and neither were you, for that matter. But the neighbor across the street told the police that she saw *you* do the crime. She was sure it was you; she even saw you arguing with the victim a few days earlier, thereby proving (in her mind) your motive to commit this crime.

Although the eyewitness thinks she's infallible, and even gave a written, signed statement to the police, you deny the allegation and demand a jury trial. At trial you will have the constitutional right to confront your accuser in court, in front of the jury. What are some things that your lawyer would want to ask this accuser, to demonstrate for the jury that her accusation is false? How about these questions, for starters: Wasn't it late at night and very dark out when you saw the perpetrator break into the garage? You weren't even wearing your glasses, were you? How far away were you? How much time did you have to observe this person? Five seconds? Isn't it true that you *initially* told police that the perpetrator was about five feet tall, and my client is well over six feet tall? You stopped drinking alcohol only an hour before you claim to have seen this, correct? How many drinks did you have? Were you drunk? Aren't you simply assuming it was the defendant because you saw him arguing with the neighbor just days earlier?

Obviously, the answers to these questions could well shed an entirely different light on the subject, metaphorically speaking. But assume for a minute that you don't have the constitutional right of confrontation. Imagine a trial where your accuser does not testify, but the jury still hears her accusation against you. Maybe she died before trial; maybe she's on vacation; maybe she doesn't want to testify; or maybe the prosecutor would rather not subpoena her for trial, because she's a perpetual drunk with a long criminal record and would hurt the state's case. Instead of live testimony, then, the police are allowed to simply read your accuser's previously written and signed statement for the jury at trial. Further, the judge instructs the jury that her statement *is* evidence that they may consider in deciding your guilt.

You might be thinking, and rightly so, that the accuser's statement would also be "hearsay," which should be excluded from evidence. However, there are now approximately thirty—that's right, thirty—exceptions to the hearsay rule. One of them is even a catch-all exception for when none of the other exceptions seem to fit. With so many broad exceptions, it is actually more accurate to say that, as a general rule, hearsay is now admissible.[3]

Going back to your hypothetical trial for burglary, the statement against you was persuasive; after all, it was drafted, reviewed, and polished by the police before your accuser signed it. And without the accuser there in court, you couldn't cross-examine her or her accusation. The jury never learned that she was drunk that night, wasn't wearing her glasses, and only had a few seconds to view something that she *thinks* she saw in the pitch black of your neighbor's yard.

You testified at trial in your own defense, and did the best you could. You denied the allegation, but you couldn't really provide any details—after all, you weren't even there. You came off as nervous, and you paled in comparison to the state's police-officer witness who convincingly read your accuser's statement to the jury. Maybe you had other drawbacks in the eyes of the jury as well, such as your race, or your prior conviction that they learned about when you testified. (Sure, it was only for a minor disorderly-conduct incident, but that fact never came out, leaving the jury to wonder what the conviction was for, and whether you had previously burglarized someone else.) On top of that, you had a motive: you were arguing with your neighbor only days earlier. For whatever reason, you lost the credibility battle in court. You were convicted of felony burglary. (Now, the real fun begins. Go back to chapter 1 for some of the things that will happen to you next.)

You can see from this simple, but extremely common example just how important cross-examination is to a fair trial. Sometimes, decent people make mistakes, and cross-examination tests the reliability of their stories and their ability to accurately perceive what they think they saw. Other times, people will have motives to lie, and cross-examination tests the credibility of the accuser. Sometimes, both of these scenarios will exist in combination, making cross-examination even more vital to a fair trial. Without cross-examination, however, the story and the storyteller would never be tested. Without cross-examination, the story and the storyteller could be accepted on mere faith, and the wrongfully accused could, quite easily, turn into the wrongfully convicted.

■ ■ ■

Now that I've illustrated the importance of cross-examination, I once again have bad news. Just like our other constitutional rights—such as the right against self-incrimination and the right to privacy in our homes—the right of confrontation is a soft law. It is extremely malleable and easily destroyed by police, prosecutors, and judges. I know what you're thinking: The constitution says that we have the right "to be confronted with the witnesses against" us.[4] This is so simple, so clear, and so uncontroversial—there's no way the government can get around this, right?

Wrong. In 1980, the U.S. Supreme Court interpreted the already clear language of the Sixth Amendment's confrontation clause.[5] When doing so, the Court realized that if the right of confrontation were read literally, and its words were given their plain and ordinary meanings, judges would be forced to exclude from evidence any accusation where the accuser was not in court for live testimony and cross-examination. At this point you might be thinking: Yes, that's the idea behind the right of confrontation. If you can't cross-examine the story and the storyteller, then the government can't use the story at trial. The prosecutor either has to get the witness into court or dismiss the case.

The government, however, didn't want that. Such a literal reading would be devastating to prosecutors all over the country, who would then have to bring the accusers into court for live testimony and cross-examination. Also, it would mean that if the prosecutor didn't want the accuser to testify, or if the accuser refused to come to court or couldn't be found, there wouldn't even be a prosecution. Therefore, the Court decided to interpret the right of confrontation less strictly and far more favorably for the government.

The Court decided that even if the accuser couldn't be in court for live testimony, the prosecutor could still have a police officer repeat the accusation at trial for the jury. The only thing the prosecutor had to do was to first ask the judge to decide that, in his or her opinion, the accusation was "reliable."[6] The judge could decide this based on any of the facts or circumstances surrounding the accusation or the way in which it was made. For example, the judge could consider the demeanor of the accuser when making the accusation, whether the accusation was made promptly or was delayed, and how much detail was given by the accuser. Where would this information come from? From the police officer who took the accuser's statement, of course.

The Supreme Court's incredibly bad ruling made it quite easy for the three arms of the government—the police, prosecutors, and judges—to sneak untested and un-cross-examined accusations into evidence against a defendant. This is best illustrated with another simple example. Assume that an alleged victim calls the police and accuses you of coming to his house, threatening him, and then battering him. You deny the allegation. Yes, you were there and argued with this guy, but you never threatened him or touched him. There's a long history of bad blood between the two of you, and he'll do and say anything if he thinks it will hurt you. So you demand a jury trial. Just before trial, however, you learn that your accuser has skipped town. Basically, he doesn't want to testify anymore. Maybe he lost interest in you; maybe he sobered up since the day of the incident; maybe he doesn't want to be cross-examined; or maybe he's a little less bold these days and is worried about perjury. No one knows for sure.

The prosecutor, however, files a motion and argues that the allegation is "reliable," and therefore he should be allowed to use it against you at trial, even without the accuser's live testimony or the opportunity for cross-examination. The judge decides to hold a pretrial hearing on this issue, before the jury trial starts. Given that the accuser in not present for testimony, all we have is the police officer's account of the accusation. The pretrial hearing on whether the statement is reliable, and therefore admissible, goes something like this:

Prosecutor: Now, Officer, did you take a statement from Mr. Victim on June 1st of this year?

Officer: Yes, I did.

Prosecutor: What did he say?

Officer: He essentially said that the defendant threatened him and battered him.

Prosecutor: Can you describe his demeanor for the judge, please?

Officer: Yes. He was very excited. He spoke quickly and frantically. He seemed very fearful, too.

Prosecutor: And did he say *when* the defendant did this to him?

Officer: Yes, he said it "just happened."

Prosecutor: And what do you remember, if anything, Officer, about the level of detail he gave?

Officer: Oh, it was a very detailed statement. Maybe the most detailed statement I'd ever taken. He told me precisely what threat was made, and told me in great detail about the battery. He was struck by the defendant's right fist.

Prosecutor: Thank you, Officer. Your Honor, based on this testimony, I move for a finding that the statement is reliable and therefore admissible as evidence at trial, even without any opportunity for cross-examination by the defendant.

Of course, *you* know this is all trumped-up, but you can't offer any testimony to refute the officer's account of the allegation; after all, you weren't there when this allegation was supposedly made. Therefore, based solely on this police officer's testimony, the judge finds the allegation to be reliable, and therefore admissible. Given that the accuser was frantic and spoke quickly—what the lawyers call an "excited utterance"—he no doubt spoke the truth; his demeanor itself, as reported by the officer, is considered to be evidence of that. (It doesn't matter that the accuser might normally speak quickly and frantically, or might have been speaking that way because he was high on coke—two things the officer would have no way of knowing, as he knew this accuser for all of five minutes.) Additionally, because the accuser reported the alleged crime soon after it happened, the judge presumes that he had no opportunity to reflect on the matter and conjure up a false allegation. (Remember, the police officer testified that the accuser had said that it "just happened.") Finally, the detailed nature of the statement also makes it credible in the eyes of the judge. (After all, the accuser even remembered which fist you used to hit him.) Therefore, given the facts and circumstances surrounding this accusation, as recounted by the police, the accusation is deemed reliable and therefore may be used against you as evidence in your trial.

The trial moves forward. Just as in the burglary example, the jury hears the accusation, as told by the police, without seeing the accuser or knowing anything about him or his possible motives for making a false allegation against you. Nor can the story itself be cross-examined or tested. Did the accuser even have any injuries? If so, couldn't they have been caused by something or someone else? Didn't he just get into a fight with someone else the day before? None of these questions will be answered. The judge made a perfunctory finding that the accusation was reliable, and the rest is a mere formality. Your right to cross-examine your accuser, no matter how fundamental to our notions of fairness, was just destroyed. Much like our burglary example, you could well find yourself convicted of a crime without your accuser ever taking the witness stand.

■ ■ ■

The Supreme Court's 1980 decision gave government agents the incredible flexibility they needed to destroy the right of confrontation. Routinely, prosecutors would offer accusations as evidence, police would testify at pretrial hearings and say all the right things, and judges would decide that the statements were reliable and therefore admissible. As a result, defendants were convicted with no opportunity for cross-examination. In time, the government agents grew so arrogant, and abused this tactic to such an extent, that court decisions started to become completely nonsensical. Instead of genuinely trying to determine which statements were really reliable—assuming that is even possible without knowing or even seeing the accuser—judges would do and say anything, no matter how ridiculous, in order to label accusations as reliable and then use them at trial.

For example, one judge would decide that an accusation was reliable, and therefore could be used by the prosecutor without cross-examination, because it was *incredibly detailed.*[7] Meanwhile, another judge would decide that an accusation was also reliable, and again could be used by the prosecutor without cross-examination, but this time because it contained *very little detail.*[8] Some judges would use any fact or circumstance, no matter how diametrically opposed the individual facts or circumstances might be to each other, in order to reach the *same* conclusion. Their only goal, along with the police and prosecutors, was to sneak untested and un-cross-examined statements into evidence. And they weren't shy about it, either.

Things really got bad when a single court would use completely opposite facts in two different cases to reach the same conclusion of reliability. For example, in one case, a court decided that a statement was reliable and therefore could be used by the prosecutor because it was made *immediately after* the alleged crime.[9] But in a different case, only a few months removed, that same court decided that a statement was reliable and could be used by the prosecutor because it was made *two years after* the alleged crime.[10] In courts like this, the right of confrontation had literally disappeared. There wasn't a set of facts or circumstances in existence that couldn't be twisted to suit the government. Every hearsay accusation was deemed reliable, and every hearsay accusation was coming into evidence.

It is interesting to imagine, for a moment, whether any other professional in any other profession could get away with what some of these judges were doing. Consider, for a moment, the medical profession. Imagine a scenario where you and your spouse were both sick and went to your doctor. You report congestion, headache, and a sore throat. The doctor says that these three symptoms are a sure sign of virus A. That sounds reasonable to you, and you get your prescription. Now it's your spouse's turn. Your spouse reports acute back and stomach pain; nothing else is wrong. The doctor says, again, that these symptoms are a sure sign of virus A. You would either think that your doctor is a quack, or, more likely, that the doctor owns stock in the drug company that makes the drug used to treat virus A. There is no way we would allow a medical professional to get away this conduct; we'd have the doctor's license taken away, and rightly so. However, for prosecutors and judges—who are also licensed professionals and are subject to disciplinary action—this type of illogical nonsense is their stock-in-trade.

Although nothing could be done for the defendants that had already been convicted based on untested hearsay allegations, prosecutorial and judicial abuse of the confrontation clause became so severe that the Supreme Court finally decided to step in and make some changes in 2004.

■ ■ ■

Although it took twenty-four years, the Supreme Court decided to put a stop to this nonsense. In so doing, the Court admitted that it had been completely misinterpreting the right of confrontation for the past twenty-five-or-so years. The Court finally realized that denying a defendant the right to cross-examine the accuser, simply because a trial judge decided that the accusation was reliable, flat-out destroyed our constitutional right. "Dispensing with cross-examination because [an accusation] is obviously reliable is akin to dispensing with jury trial because a defendant is obviously guilty. This is not what the [right of confrontation] prescribes."[11] The Court further admitted, based on decades of judicial abuse by lower courts, that "judges, like other government agents, could not always be trusted to safeguard the rights of the people."[12] So the Court decided that from that point forward, the reliability of accusations must be decided by juries, not by judges, and only after confrontation in court—that is, "testing in the crucible of cross-examination."[13]

The Court made an exception to this new rule, however. There were some statements collected by police, the Court believed, that were so far removed from the risk of manipulation by police, prosecutors, and judges that they *could* be used at trial, even without the opportunity for cross-examination. These accusations were those that were made for the "primary purpose" of helping the police to resolve an "ongoing emergency."[14] The new rule and its exception are best explained with a simple example of a 9-1-1 emergency phone call.

Police: This is 9-1-1, what is your emergency?

Accuser: My sister is crazy! She came at me and punched me with her fist, and she said she is going to do it again. She's in the house with me somewhere. Send help, fast!

Police: Okay, okay, just stay calm. What is your name, your sister's name, and where do you live?

Accuser: My name is Anna. My sister's name is Betsy. I'm at 1111 Lakeshore Drive. Hurry! I see her in the living room, and she's coming at me. Hurry!

Police: Okay, calm down, a squad has been dispatched. Get to a safe place in the house. Where is Betsy now?

Accuser: She saw that I was on the phone and she ran out the door. I can see her driving away now with her friend Cathy in Cathy's car. She's headed south on Lakeshore Drive.

Police: Okay, but we're still sending a squad car. They just pulled up outside your house, and they're on their way in. Stay on the line with me until they arrive. Now, has anything like this ever happened before?

Accuser: Yes. Just yesterday Betsy hit me in the head with a baseball bat. She came up behind me and smacked me a good one. It really, really hurt. Then I lost consciousness for a few minutes. Okay, the police just walked in my house. Thanks, bye.

Here's how the Court's new rule would work under this set of facts: Because Anna's primary purpose in making her call was to get help, and *not* to accuse Betsy of a crime, her accusation about being punched was made in the course of an ongoing emergency. As a result, this accusation could legally be used by the prosecutor at Betsy's trial, even if Anna, the accuser, didn't show up for cross-examination. However, the Court also made clear that once the ongoing emergency ended—here, when Betsy drove off in the car with her friend Cathy—any accusation after that point in time obviously was *not* part of an ongoing emergency. Therefore, Anna's accusation that Betsy hit her with a baseball bat the day before could *not* be used at trial, *unless* Anna was present in court for cross-examination regarding that accusation.

This new rule, as well as the clearly articulated policy behind it, seemed very straightforward and appeared to put an end to the government's abuse of our constitutional right of confrontation. Unfortunately, however, this new rule turned out to be mere putty in the hands of police, prosecutors, and judges. It proved to be as soft and malleable as the Supreme Court's old reliability test from 1980. How were the government agents able to bypass this new and improved right of confrontation? Much like putting a square peg into a round hole, they forced any and all accusations into the realm of an ongoing emergency, by simply expanding the scope of the emergency.

In our last example—with Anna the accuser, and her sister Betsy the defendant—assume that the prosecutor is reviewing the case, and he really wants to charge Betsy with a felony. Further, Anna now refuses to testify; she no longer wants to prosecute her sister. Maybe Anna made up the accusation; maybe she exaggerated it; or maybe everything was true, but her sister is now getting psychiatric help and Anna wants to drop the charges, although the state refuses to do so. Whatever the reason, the prosecutor is left without an accusing witness. However, at trial the prosecutor could still use the first accusation—the one about being punched by Betsy—because that was made during the course of an ongoing emergency.

The prosecutor realizes, however, that the punching accusation is only good enough to get a misdemeanor. In order to get a felony charge, the prosecutor really needs to use that second accusation, where Anna accused Betsy of knocking her out cold with a baseball bat. (The prosecutor knows that an accusation of battery that results in unconsciousness is a felony.) But the problem for the prosecutor is that the baseball bat accusation was not made until *after* Betsy left the apartment and the emergency had ended. So how does the prosecutor get around that roadblock? By expanding the ongoing emergency, like this:

Prosecutor: Your Honor, although the victim, Anna, is not present for trial, the state intends to use *both* of her accusations, including the accusation that the defendant, Betsy, struck her with a baseball bat and knocked her unconscious.

Defense Lawyer: Judge, the baseball-bat allegation was made *after* the defendant left the apartment and the police arrived at the house. Any emergency was over at that point. This accusation was therefore not part of an ongoing emergency, and cannot be used by the prosecutor unless we can cross-examine it, which we can't because the accuser is not here.

Prosecutor: Judge, that's not true. At the time the baseball-bat allegation was made, it was not known *exactly* where the defendant was. In fact, the police were only in the area, not yet inside the house with the victim. Therefore, the attack could have conceivably been renewed before the police were able to help.

Defense Lawyer: Judge, that's nonsense. The police were right outside. The defendant was long gone in a car, heading in the other direction. The Supreme Court said that once the defendant drives away, the emergency ends. The baseball-bat accusation, therefore, cannot be used unless we have the opportunity for cross examination, which we don't.

Judge: Mr. Defense Lawyer, as you well know, that statement by the Supreme Court was *dicta*, that is, not central to its holding under the immediate set of facts before it; therefore, I don't need to follow it. I like the prosecutor's argument. This emergency hadn't necessarily fully subsided. Therefore, until the moment the police entered the home, *every-*

thing was part of an ongoing emergency. And because both accusations were made *before* that point in time, they were both made in the course of the ongoing emergency. All accusations are therefore admissible, and the defendant will stand trial on the felony charge.

Does that seem like an incredible stretch? Well, it actually happened, nearly word for word, in a real case.[15] But let's change the facts a bit. Let's say that the prosecutor is really unlucky. Suppose that Anna had made the baseball bat accusation just *after* the police walked into her home. What then? The judge just said that once the police entered the home, the emergency ended. The baseball-bat accusation would therefore *not* be part of an ongoing emergency, and would not be admissible, even under the trial judge's distorted view of the law. The prosecutor is sunk, right? Not yet. Here's what could, and has, happened:

Prosecutor: Your Honor, the state intends to use *both* of the victim's accusations, including the baseball-bat accusation.

Defense Lawyer: Judge, the baseball-bat accusation was made after the defendant left, *and even after the police entered the home to protect the alleged victim.* Any emergency had long ended by that point.

Prosecutor: Judge, that's not true. At the time the baseball-bat allegation was made, the defendant had left in a car with Cathy. Perhaps Cathy was in danger. The statements that were made after the police arrived were helpful in assessing the situation, and protecting *all* potential victims, not just Anna.

Defense Lawyer: Judge, that's nonsense. The Supreme Court said that once the police arrive, the emergency has ended. If you rule in favor of the prosecutor, then *every accusation* will become part of an ongoing emergency; in theory, it's always possible that a defendant could commit an unspecified crime against an unidentified person at some undetermined time in the future. It's got nothing to do with the emergency in this case, and we all know that.

Judge: Mr. Defense Lawyer, as you well know, that statement by the Supreme Court was, again, dicta, and I'm not bound by it. Besides, nothing in the law says that the emergency has to be limited to the present victim or the present location. There very well could have been a threat to *Cathy's* safety, in the car, at the time the victim made her baseball-bat allegation against the defendant. The questioning by police could reason-

ably have been intended to assess an ongoing emergency to other victims
at other locations. Therefore, all accusations may come in, and the defendant will stand trial on the felony charge.

This judicial ruling just distorted the concept of an ongoing emergency beyond all recognition, and obliterated the right of confrontation in the process.[16] Much like the good-faith exception to the warrant requirement from
chapter 5, everything now satisfies the exception to the rule, and the rule
itself is swallowed whole. But these examples don't even begin to describe
the lengths to which police and prosecutors will go in order to bypass the
Constitution. In fact, police, with the help of prosecutors, will actually design
and structure their investigations well ahead of time in order to later defeat
the right of confrontation in court.

Consider this example: Tami, a college cheerleader, claims that Tommy,
a college sports star, had sex with her against her will at a college party.
Now, we all know that in reality, people are sexually assaulted. We also
know that many sexual assaults are never even reported, let alone prosecuted.
However, we also know that sometimes people make false allegations of
sexual assault; after all, the Duke Lacrosse scandal is still a recent memory.[17]
In our case, it turns out that Tami and Tommy, both adult college students,
did have sex, but Tommy claims it was consensual. Further, the sex act didn't
mean as much to Tommy as it did to Tami, and he moved on to another
woman rather quickly. Tami didn't like that, and was going to make Tommy
pay. After she got drunk and angry one night, she went to the police. With a
case like this, however, the police know that come time for jury trial, Tami
may not want to pursue this accusation with the same vigor that she exhibits
in her drunken and angry state at the police station. So what do the police do?
It's simple, actually.

The police will call the prosecutor's office to explain the situation. The
prosecutor instructs the police *not* to get involved, but rather to send Tami
directly to a nurse at the state-funded trauma center for rape victims. The
nurse physically examines Tami and also video-records her detailed accusation. But as the prosecutor already knew, the nurse is a "mandatory reporter."[18] That means that she is required by law to turn the video-recorded
accusation over to the police. The police will then give that videotape to the
prosecutor, who will file charges.

If Tami later decides that it really wasn't rape and therefore refuses to
testify at Tommy's trial, it really doesn't matter. Why? Because the police
sent Tami to the nurse, which allows the judge to find that Tami's accusation
was made for the purpose of obtaining medical assistance, and *not* to report a
crime. Therefore, the prosecutor can play the videotaped accusation for the

jury at Tommy's trial, even without any opportunity to cross-examine Tami.[19] The accuser and the accusation will be untested, and might be accepted on mere faith.

Pretty creative, isn't it? If you look at the substance rather than the form of what just happened, this is nothing more than a cheaply constructed veil used to hide accusations from our right of confrontation. All the government did was use a middleman—in this case, the nurse—to do the job of the police. It was she, instead of the police, who videotaped the accusation. Then, the police got the recorded accusation anyway because the government nurse was required, by law, to turn it over to police. This simple tactic, employed ahead of time for the specific purpose of bypassing the Constitution, is enough to give a judge something on which to hang his or her hat and rule that the statement was *not* made for the purpose of reporting a crime, but rather for medical purposes. With that ruling, the prosecutor is allowed to use the accusation without any opportunity for cross-examination by the defendant.

■ ■ ■

The blatant and intentional abuses of the right of confrontation discussed in this chapter should terrify each and every one of us. It is true that *some* constitutional rights, such as the right to privacy, can be directly at odds with the substantive criminal law, as demonstrated by the marijuana-cigarette example in chapter 2. In such cases, many argue that, because a factually guilty person was ultimately convicted, the ends (convictions of guilty people) justified the means (violating constitutional rights). Although we know that this argument is flawed, and that such thinking is, in fact, very dangerous for all of us, it does hold some superficial appeal.

With the right of confrontation, however, this flawed argument completely loses its already minimal value. In the Tami-Tommy example, unlike the marijuana-cigarette example, there is no reason to even suspect the defendant is guilty, except for the accusation itself. If the accusation is used at trial but cannot be cross-examined, and the defendant is found guilty, then a presumably innocent person—maybe your parent, maybe your spouse, or maybe even you—has been convicted solely on an untested accusation. It is mind-boggling how our government agents would even *want* to prosecute and convict any citizen with un-cross-examined accusations, let alone why they would go to such extravagant lengths to do so.

■ ■ ■

Before we explore other constitutional rights, the next chapter will take a momentary step back, away from the fray, and discuss some basics of criminal procedure. Hopefully, it will also dispel some legal myths in the process.

NOTES

1. "In all criminal prosecutions, the accused shall enjoy the right . . . to be confronted with the witnesses against him . . ." United States Constitution, Sixth Amendment, at www.law.cornell.edu/constitution/sixth_amendment (accessed November 3, 2011).

2. For an example of a rape-shield law, see Wis. Stat. sec. 972.11(2), at docs.legis.wisconsin.gov/statutes/statutes/972.pdf (accessed November 3, 2011).

3. For an example of the general rule against hearsay, as well as its voluminous exceptions, see Wis. Stat. Ch. 908, at docs.legis.wisconsin.gov/statutes/statutes/908.pdf (accessed November 3, 2011).

4. U.S. Constitution, Sixth Amendment.

5. *Ohio v. Roberts*, 448 U.S. 56 (1980).

6. Ibid.

7. *People v. Farrell*, 34 P.3d 401 (Colo. 2001).

8. *U.S. v. Photogrammetric Data Services*, 259 F.3d 229 (4th Cir. 2001; finding a statement reliable because it "was fleeting at best").

9. *People v. Farrell*, 34 P.3d 401 (Colo. 2001).

10. *Stevens v. People*, 29 P.3d 305 (Colo. 2001).

11. *Crawford v. Washington*, 541 U.S. 36 (2004).

12. Ibid.

13. Ibid.

14. *Davis v. Washington*, 126 S. Ct. 2266 (2006).

15. *State v. Camarena*, 145 P.3d 267 (Ore. Ct. App. 2006).

16. *State v. Warsame*, 723 N.W.2d 637 (Minn. Ct. App. 2006).

17. Duff Wilson and David Barstow, "All Charges Dropped in Duke Case," *New York Times*, April 12, 2007, at www.nytimes.com/2007/04/12/us/12duke.html?ref=dukelacrossesexualassaultcase (accessed November 6, 2011).

18. Failure to comply with this law could result in criminal charges against the mandatory reporter, an issue central to the Penn State football investigation and the Syracuse University basketball investigation. These investigations have resulted in a flurry of legislation by lawmakers who are eager to grab the spotlight in the wake of these two so-called scandals. See, for example, "State Law Maker Demands Mandatory Reporting of Sex Abuse Claims," *CBS Chicago.com*, November 23, 2011, at chicago.cbslocal.com/2011/11/23/state-lawmaker-demands-mandatory-reporting-of-sex-abuse-claims/ (accessed November 24, 2011).

19. *In the Matter of A.J.A.*, 2006 Minn. App. Lexis 988 (2006).

Chapter Seven

Taking a Step Back

Some Procedural Basics

Our discussion so far—about the right against self-incrimination, the right of privacy, and the right of confrontation—has hopefully cleared up a lot of misconceptions about the criminal justice system and our constitutional rights. However, we may have raised some new, more practical questions in the process, particularly the following: (1) Can't an accuser just drop the charges and dismiss the case against a defendant? (2) How can the state prosecute a defendant based merely on allegations, and without any evidence? (3) When ruling on a defendant's motions, such as a motion to suppress a defendant's alleged confession, how does the judge know what really happened or what was really said?

In this chapter we'll take a temporary step back, away from the specific, substantive constitutional rights, to resolve these three new issues.

■ ■ ■

When studying the right of confrontation in chapter 6, we learned that sometimes alleged victims will accuse a person of a crime, but then decide that they don't want the person prosecuted. In these cases, the accuser may change or recant his or her story, or simply refuse to testify altogether. There are, of course, many possible reasons for such a change of heart. Maybe the accuser now realizes that the government is trying to convict and punish, rather than rehabilitate, the accused. Or maybe the accuser actually lied when making the original accusation, and now doesn't want to follow through and commit perjury at trial. The possible reasons are endless.

Regardless of why an accuser changes his or her mind, you may be asking the very same thing that many of my clients ask me: Can't the accuser just drop the charges and make the case go away? The answer is a resounding no. The accuser—the person whom prosecutors and many judges have anointed as "the victim" long before anything is ever proved in court—is simply *not* a party to the criminal case.

A criminal case, in many ways, is just like a civil lawsuit that is filed by a private party. For example, if Jenny sues Johnny for breach of contract on a business deal gone bad, the parties to the civil lawsuit are Jenny, the plaintiff, and Johnny, the defendant. If Jenny wishes, she can drop the civil case at any time, or settle it under any terms she wants to which Johnny will agree. But if Jenny accuses Johnny of having illegal sexual contact with her—or if she accuses him of any other crime, for that matter—it's an entirely different story. In that case, the parties to the criminal case are the state (the plaintiff) and Johnny (the defendant). Sometimes the plaintiff in the criminal complaint will be called "the people" or "the commonwealth"; however, the important point is that Jenny is *not* the plaintiff and therefore cannot drop the charges. In fact, she never pressed charges to begin with; she only made an accusation. It is the state government—or in a federal case, the federal government—that filed the criminal complaint and initiated the lawsuit against the defendant. Only the state, and not Jenny or any other accuser, can dismiss it.

Nearly every state has a myriad of victim-rights laws, giving the accuser all kinds of rights and powers throughout the course of a defendant's criminal case, and even beyond. But those rights are only meaningful in cases where the accuser *agrees* with the state's decision to prosecute the defendant. The minute the accuser wants to drop the charges, his or her interests diverge from those of the state and, at that point, the so-called victim's rights become far less potent. In reality, it is the state, not the alleged victim, who runs the show. The alleged victim is merely a witness, and, as we saw in chapter 6, the state is even able, in many circumstances, to prosecute and convict a defendant without any cooperation or testimony from that witness, despite the defendant's constitutional right of confrontation.

The important point to remember is that once the accuser makes that phone call to the police, the incident is no longer a family matter or an issue among friends. Now the state is involved; and once the state has been invited to the dance, it usually doesn't leave willingly.

■ ■ ■

The second issue that you might be wondering about, and one that was briefly addressed in chapter 2 where Jenny accused Johnny of sexual assault, is the issue of evidence. In other words, what *is* evidence? I've had numerous clients march into my office, with their criminal complaints in hand, and demand that I get their cases thrown out because there is no evidence against them. All the state has is an accusation, they protest. Other descriptive terminology, often uttered out of the frustration of being accused of a crime, includes "hearsay" or "he said—she said."

First, the state doesn't need any evidence at the time of filing the criminal complaint and setting the so-called wheels of justice into motion. All they need is an accusation, and that accusation can even be secondhand, or hearsay.[1] Consider this modified excerpt from an actual but awkwardly worded criminal complaint:

> John Jones, the defendant, is an adult male who resides in the aforementioned city, county and state. While at his residence in the evening hours of July 1, 2007, the defendant was present with his son, Jacob J., date of birth July 1, 2000. On July 2, 2007, Jacob J. came to the city police station with his mother and reported that, on July 1, 2007 while at the defendant's residence, and in the defendant's bedroom, the defendant yelled at him, which scared Jacob J. The defendant then struck Jacob J. with a closed fist, seven or eight times, on right side of the face, causing him pain. Jacob J. then reports that the defendant pushed him into the bedroom door, causing him to hit his face on the door, and to fall backwards onto the defendant's bed. The force of the defendant's actions then caused Jacob J. to roll off the bed and onto a water fountain, causing more pain. Jacob J.'s mother, Jenny Jones, reports that she took Jacob J. to the emergency room for a full evaluation where no physical injuries were detected. Jenny Jones further reports that she saw no injuries on Jacob J. at any time on or after July 1, 2007.

In this case, based on these factual allegations from the criminal complaint, the state charged John Jones with disorderly conduct and, worse yet, two counts of felony child abuse for the alleged violence against his son, Jacob J.[2] Further, from the time the state files the criminal complaint up to the time that the jury trial begins, all allegations in the complaint, no matter how ridiculous, are presumed by law to be factually true. Unlike the presumptions that we discussed in the context of search warrants in chapter 5, however, the defendant has virtually no opportunity to rebut this presumption. Disputes as to what actually happened are issues to be saved for trial.

Usually, in a case like the one described above against John Jones, a defendant's only chance to get a criminal complaint dismissed before trial is to show that the factual allegations, even when taken as true, cannot possibly constitute the crime charged. To use an obvious example, John Jones's complaint, above, could not support a charge of homicide because there is no allegation that anyone died; however, it could support numerous other charges, like child abuse, battery, reckless endangerment, and disorderly conduct, to name only a few.

But even when the complaint is legally defective, getting a commissioner or judge to actually dismiss it (or parts of it) is an intense battle. And, worse yet, any dismissal would be without prejudice, meaning that the prosecutor can simply redraft the complaint, fix the defects, and file it again. And again after that. And, generally speaking, as many times as is needed until he or she gets it right.

Going back to the John Jones example, the complaint only has to allege two things—which, again, will be presumed to be true—in order to support the allegation of felony child abuse: first, that the defendant caused some injury or pain to the alleged victim; and, second, that the alleged victim was under the age of eighteen. Here, the complaint satisfies both of those elements by stating that Jacob J. reported "pain," and by providing Jacob J.'s date of birth as well as the date of the alleged crimes, from which his age at the time of the incident can be deduced. Therefore, since both elements are properly alleged, and are presumed to be true no matter how ridiculous and improbable they are, the complaint is valid and will not be dismissed. Yes, the law also says that the defendant must *intentionally* cause the pain, but that will simply be assumed in most cases, especially when the complaint alleges an intentional act like punching.

Staying with the abbreviated criminal complaint against John Jones, then, it doesn't matter that everyone—except, apparently, the prosecutor—knows that eight punches to a child's face by an adult male would leave a mark or bruise of some kind, but here there was none. Neither does it matter that slamming a child's face into a door would also cause some type of visible injury, but again, here there was none. Finally, neither does it matter that the child wasn't even at the home on July 1st, the day of the alleged crime, or that the bedroom door is nowhere near the bed, or that there isn't even a "fountain" in the yard, let alone in the bedroom, onto which the child could fall. None of that matters, because the factual allegations in the complaint are presumed to be true.

But what about evidence *at trial*? Doesn't the state eventually have to put on some actual evidence? Well, yes, but an accusation *is* evidence. Whether it's believable is ultimately up to the jury, but an accusation, even by itself, is considered evidence.[3] In fact, the prosecutor wouldn't even need actual, live testimony to prove its case against John Jones in the above example. How is that? In many child-victim allegations, including alleged physical abuse, the state will have video-recorded the child's initial accusation. Come time for the state to prove its case at trial, all the prosecutor has to do is pop in the videocassette and press "play."[4] Then, to satisfy John Jones's constitutional right of confrontation, the prosecutor will plop the child on the witness stand and let John Jones's lawyer ask him questions. Of course, by the time John Jones gets to trial months or years later, the child won't even remember the allegation, which was nothing more than a bizarre fantasy anyway.[5] Good luck with cross-examination.

In the real-life case of our hypothetical John Jones, the allegation was so preposterous that it was eventually dismissed by the prosecutor. Unfortunately, the prosecutor waited until three days before trial and only decided to dismiss it when he finally realized that he wasn't able to extort a plea to a lesser charge. The prosecutor no doubt suspected that if he hadn't dismissed it, there weren't twelve prospective jurors alive anywhere who would have convicted John Jones, or any other defendant, based on those absurd allegations.

However, even though things eventually worked out for John Jones, his case illuminates two distinct problems for the broader legal system. The first problem is that prosecutors can, and do, file criminal complaints recklessly, under the motto "charge now, investigate later." This approach makes things incredibly easy for the prosecutor, but places an enormous emotional and financial burden on the accused citizen and society in general. For example, when a prosecutor waits until three days before trial to dismiss a case that never should have been filed in the first place, the defendant has spent many months of his or her life living under restrictive bond conditions—often including no contact with family—and many thousands of dollars in attorney's fees and other costs. The prosecutor, however, answers to no one, and is not responsible for any of the financial or emotional disaster caused by his or her recklessness. Further, if the defendant is indigent, then the taxpayers of the county or state will bear the financial burden. The citizens will have to pay not only for the routine costs associated with a courthouse clogged by frivolous criminal complaints, but also for each indigent defendant's attorney's fees and other costs, including housing and feeding the defendant in the local jail while he or she awaits trial.

The second and more serious problem of prosecuting without actual evidence arises when false allegations are, on their face, plausible. Again, in the John Jones case, the allegations almost proved their own falsity; that is, the allegations were, on their face, so highly implausible, if not physically impossible, that few people outside of the prosecutor's office would ever believe them. But what if a false allegation is physically possible or, worse yet, even plausible? In that case, because the accusation is, by itself, considered to be evidence, an innocent person can be convicted on that alone.

For example, instead of the bizarre and highly improbable accusation from our previous example, what if Jacob J. had simply said that John Jones had touched him in a bad place? Because there is no physical evidence or lack of physical evidence to prove or disprove such an allegation, there is a much greater chance that jurors will want to believe it and convict John Jones, even without any real evidence to support it. In fact, some jurors, either consciously or subconsciously, may shift the burden of proof to the defendant when an accusation is, on its face, plausible. Instead of asking if the state has proved the allegation beyond a reasonable doubt, they may instead ask, "Why would Jacob J. lie?" And if they didn't think to ask that question, the prosecutor will ask it for them, rhetorically, in the closing argument. And therein lies the real danger of our criminal justice system. [6]

■ ■ ■

Another question that you might be asking after reading the earlier chapters is this: How does the judge makes his or her findings of fact? In other words, when a defendant asks the judge to suppress evidence because the police violated constitutional rights, how does the judge know what really happened and what was really said? We have seen how police, prosecutors, and judges can take virtually any set of facts and manipulate them to reach any conclusion they want. But where do these underlying facts actually come from?

For example, if a defendant tries to exclude evidence recovered in what *she* claims was an illegal search of her home, how does the judge know that the defendant really said, "I give you consent to search my home"? Or, if a defendant tries to exclude his statement from evidence because the police didn't honor his *Miranda* rights, how does the judge know that the defendant really said "*maybe* I should get a lawyer" as opposed to "I *demand* a lawyer this instant"? Or, if a defendant tries to exclude a witness's allegation because the witness isn't present at trial for cross-examination, how does the judge know that the witness really spoke frantically and appeared afraid when he initially accused the defendant? More importantly, how do we know that the alleged victim even accused the defendant at all?

In some cases, as we have seen, these events are intentionally recorded on video or audio. For example, accusers' 9-1-1 calls are often recorded and preserved on audio, so the judge will know exactly what was said. The recording tells nothing about the *truthfulness* of what was said; but unless the tape was somehow altered, which would be unusual, the judge will know *what* was said. As another example, a few states now require police to video-record interrogations of suspects. In these cases, there is again an objective, verifiable statement. Granted, the suspect's confession may still have been coerced, and it may even be factually false, but at least the judge will know, for the most part, what the defendant actually said, and when and how it was said.

But in reality, most cases aren't nearly this clear-cut. In most cases, the actual facts are uncertain. Therefore, when the judges make their findings of fact, which they must do before they can rule on a defendant's motion to suppress or exclude evidence, they will simply accept as true whatever version of events the police tell them. In many cases, there won't even be anything to contradict the police version of events, leaving the judge with no real decision to make.

Cases involving the right of confrontation are good examples of this. As we saw in chapter 6, these cases arise when the prosecutor asks a police officer to repeat an accusation instead of calling the accuser for live testimony. Of course, because the accuser is not in court, *he* cannot tell the jury what he really said, or whether he felt scared or threatened by the defendant when he said it. Further, it would be highly unusual for a defendant to witness an accusation being made against him or her. Therefore, unless the accusation happened to be in the form of a 9-1-1 call, the only person who can testify about *what* was supposedly said, *who* supposedly said it, and *when* and *how* the accuser supposedly said it is the police officer. There is usually nothing to contradict the officer's version of events, no matter how self-serving it is, and the judge will simply accept it as true.

In other cases, the defendant *will* be able to provide the judge with a conflicting version of events. For example, if the issue is whether the police illegally entered the defendant's home before finding the evidence—say, a marijuana cigarette—then the defendant could certainly testify. While the officer would testify that the defendant gave permission for entering the home, the defendant might testify that the officer entered the home *without* consent. But, in cases like that, who do you think the judge is going to believe? The police officer, who testifies in the judge's court on a regular basis and diligently protects the community from wrongdoing? Or the defendant, who breaks the law by keeping marijuana cigarettes in the house? Unless these actual events were somehow unknowingly recorded, you can bet that the judge will, nearly every single time, rubber-stamp the officer's version of what happened.

It is bad enough that police, prosecutors, and judges are able to manipulate already existing facts to their liking; we've already seen that in numerous contexts. But now, we also know that in many cases it is these same government agents who get to decide what the facts *are* in the first place This power gives them the ability to recreate the facts as they want them to be, rather than as they really happened. Put in a less diplomatic way, they can simply lie.

How do we know this? There are at least two ways. First, in rare cases there is direct evidence of it. Sometimes the police will lie—whether in their written reports or, even better, under oath in pretrial hearings—and, unbeknownst to them, the event about which they are testifying was actually recorded on video or audio. This doesn't happen often, but defendants may find themselves on the receiving end of such good fortune from time to time. In one case, for example, a female defendant had called the police to report that *she* had been beaten by her husband. The police responded to her house, but for some reason they just didn't like her, or didn't want to arrest her husband. Instead, the police ended up arresting *her*, and charging her with two crimes: first, obstructing an officer, for allegedly admitting to police that she'd lied about the beating, even though her booking photo later showed she had severe facial injuries; and, second, disorderly conduct, for allegedly throwing a tantrum when the police arrested her instead of her husband.

What the responding police officer didn't realize, however, is that when the woman had called 9-1-1 to initially report the battery by her husband, the 9-1-1 operator made her stay on the line until the police arrived. All of these 9-1-1 calls are, of course, recorded. Further, after the police arrived at her residence, the woman forgot to hang up the phone, and the entire exchange with the police officer was unknowingly recorded. This audio recording proved that the woman did *not* admit to lying about having been beaten (which defeated the obstructing an officer charge), and also that she was completely calm and polite the entire time (which defeated the disorderly conduct charge). The recording also captured the opposite of what the police officer had claimed: it was the police officer who was screaming and yelling. Of course, because the police officer never knew this was recorded, he never bothered to destroy the evidence. All of it was recorded on audio, and the prosecutor had no choice but to (eventually) dismiss the criminal charges against the woman.

Although many police officers consider their lying to be a badge of honor, and have even coined the phrase "testilying" for when they lie under oath,[7] rarely does such hard evidence against the police come out during the course of a case. And even when it does, usually nothing at all is done about it. In most cases, the best a defendant can hope for is a dismissal of the charges against *her*, and not disciplinary action against the police. The reason for this is that not only do the police lie, but some prosecutors, and even some judges, know it, and accept it as part of the criminal justice system. Therefore, it's not at all alarming to them when it happens.[8]

This phenomenon of police perjury has been widely studied. A very interesting case study was done in the context of the exclusionary rule—the rule discussed in chapter 5 that sometimes excludes from trial evidence obtained in violation of our privacy rights.[9] This rule was first applied to state-police officers in 1961; before then, state-police officers could simply stop anyone they wanted, for any or no reason at all, and search each of them. If the police happened to find contraband, they would arrest the person and then write a police report about it. Because there was no incentive to lie, most police officers simply wrote what really happened: they stopped a suspect for no reason at all, reached into his or her pocket, and found the contraband. There was nothing improper about that practice, so there was no incentive to lie about it.

After 1961, however, the U.S. Supreme Court decided that the state police needed a legally valid reason to stop and search a person. Based on that ruling, something changed, but it wasn't that the number of random searches decreased in order to comply with the new constitutional requirement. Instead, what changed was that police officers would simply lie to justify their searches. Instead of simply writing in their reports, as they did before, that suspects were stopped and were searched for no reason, they started writing something different. In 50 percent of the reports that were studied, police wrote that the contraband just magically fell out of suspects' pockets, thereby creating a legally valid reason to arrest them.

Obviously, contraband didn't just start dropping out of pockets merely because of the new Supreme Court ruling. Everyone knew that, but it didn't matter. These trumped-up facts about falling contraband were then repeated by police, under oath, at suppression hearings, where their perjury defeated defendants' claims of privacy-rights violations. "The exclusionary rule was having a strong impact on police behavior . . . it was encouraging false testimony to make it appear the police were conforming to the Fourth Amendment."[10] And the prosecutors and judges were all too eager to accept it.

But lying isn't always that easy, and sometimes a police officer and a prosecutor will get their signals crossed. Sometimes the police officer might take the witness stand in a pretrial evidentiary hearing and mistakenly tell the truth. Don't worry for the prosecutor, though; the judge will be there to bail the prosecutor out and find a way to admit the evidence. Consider this example, taken nearly word for word from the transcript of a real-life suppression hearing. In this hearing, the defendant was arguing that his statement should be suppressed because, at the time the police interrogated him, he was in custody and had not been read his *Miranda* rights. The key issue at this hearing, then, is whether the defendant was "free to go" at the time he was being interrogated.

Prosecutor: In the course of your investigation, did you question the defendant?

Officer: Yes, I did.

Prosecutor: When you questioned him, was he free to go?

Officer: (No response.)

Prosecutor: Officer, when you questioned him, was he free to go?

Officer: No, he wasn't free to go.

Prosecutor: He was *not*?!

Defense Lawyer: Objection, Judge, the question has already been asked and answered.

Judge: Let him clarify it. Overruled.

Defense Lawyer: Judge, it's clear from his answer and the prosecutor's surprised recital of his answer that it was not the answer that the prosecutor was looking for. The court is just giving him an opportunity to change that answer.

Judge: Well, "non-responsiveness" is not the appropriate objection, so I'm overruling your objection.

Defense Lawyer: Judge, I didn't make a "non-responsiveness" objection. My objection was "asked and answered."

Judge: (Frustrated.) I just want the truth of what happened here. Officer, answer the question again.

Officer: I mean, I did *not* have him detained at that time.

Prosecutor: Nothing further, Judge.

Defense Lawyer: Officer, when you were first questioned by the prosecutor whether the defendant was free to go, you said no. Do you remember saying that?

Officer: Yes, I did say that. I made a mistake. He—he *was* free to go.

Judge: OK, I'm ready to rule. I recognize the apparent inconsistency of the officer's responses to this question. However, he is the only witness with respect to this issue, and he said he was mistaken. So, the defendant was not in custody at the time he was being interrogated. The *Miranda* warnings were not necessary, and there was no *Miranda* violation.

Seriously, it was that easy. Even when a police officer fails to read *Miranda* warnings, he or she can fix it in court. And even when the officer gets confused and forgets how he or she is supposed to answer—after all, there's a fifty percent chance of getting it wrong—the prosecutor can just ask the question again. And even when the defense lawyer attempts to rein in this blatant fraud, the judge can step in and bail the police and the prosecutor out. Again, a constitutional right is mere putty in the hands of government agents.

■ ■ ■

Now that we've addressed these three procedural points—whether the accuser can drop the charges (answer: no); whether someone can be convicted on an accusation alone (answer: yes); and how the judge makes findings of facts at evidentiary hearings (answer: the police will tell the judge)—we will now return to the world of constitutional criminal law, and explore some additional, substantive constitutional rights, starting with the right to a speedy trial.

NOTES

1. For a discussion of the legal standard for a criminal complaint, see *State v. Williamson*, 325 N.W.2d 360 (Wis. Ct. App. 1982).

2. For an example of a child-abuse crime, see Wisconsin Statutes section 948.03, at docs.legis.wisconsin.gov/statutes/statutes/948.pdf (accessed November 5, 2011).

3. For an example of a judicial instruction to the jury that defines "evidence" to include the testimony of witnesses, see Wisconsin Jury Instructions—Criminal, no. 103 (Madison: Continuing Legal Education for Wisconsin, University of Wisconsin Law School, 2011).

4. For an example of a statute allowing the state to use video-recorded testimony in its case-in-chief, see Wisconsin Statute section 908.08, at docs.legis.wisconsin.gov/statutes/statutes/908.pdf (accessed November 5, 2011). For a case upholding the constitutionality of this trial tactic, see *State v. James,* 2005 WI App. 188.

5. The right of confrontation, when enforced, may be satisfied simply by having the witness sit in the witness chair, even if he or she can't remember anything or is unable (or unwilling) to answer questions about the incident. See *California v. Green*, 399 U.S. 149 (1970).

6. For a horrifying example showing how easy it is to be convicted of sexual assault of a child, see *State v. Brown*, 2008 Wisc. App. LEXIS 189, where the jury convicted the defendant of sexually assaulting the child based solely on the child's allegation that he was in bed, asleep, and never woke up for the assault, but knew he was assaulted and knew that it wasn't a dream because he actually had other dreams that night.

7. Albert W. Alschuler, "Studying the Exclusionary Rule: An Empirical Classic," 75 *University of Chicago Law Review* 1365 (2008).

8. In fairness, I am aware of one case of police perjury where the prosecutor immediately disclosed it and then asked the police officer to voluntarily resign or, in the alternative, face perjury charges. (If only the rest of us had such a get-out-of-jail-free card.) Conversely, I am also aware of a case where a police officer testified contrary to a defendant's interest but then, to his credit, admitted on cross-examination that he testified that way after the prosecutor had told him, during their pretrial meeting, that the pro-defendant version of events contained in his police report posed a problem for the state's case. (It didn't take long for the jury to acquit the defendant on all charges.)

9.   See Gerald F. Uelmen, *Lessons from the Trial: The People v. O.J. Simpson* (Notable Trials Library, 2003); and Gabriel J. Chin and Scott C. Wells, "The Blue Wall of Silence as Evidence of Bias and Motive to Lie: A New Approach to Police Perjury," 59 *University of Pittsburg Law Review* 233, 249 (1998).

10.   Uelmen, *Lessons from the Trial*, 39.

Chapter Eight

You Have the Right to a (Speedy) Trial

The Constitution guarantees that every citizen charged with a crime has the right to a speedy trial.[1] A speedy trial can be of the utmost importance for a number of reasons. Most significantly, when a citizen is charged with a crime and is awaiting trial, he or she will either be incarcerated or, if able to post bail, subjected to very restrictive conditions of release. These conditions of release, or bond conditions, are wide-ranging and will control where he or she can go, what he or she can do, and whom he or she can see. If the defendant violates one of these bond conditions—for example, by having a phone call with the alleged crime victim in violation of a "no contact" order, or by drinking a can of beer in violation of a "no alcohol" condition—the defendant will be charged with additional crimes known as bail jumping.

There are other reasons that a quick resolution of a case can be very important to a defendant. As time drags on in a criminal case, valuable defense witnesses may move out of the state, or their memories may fade, never again to be recovered. Additionally, and not insignificantly, criminal allegations can cause tremendous anxiety for a defendant; in many cases, an accused citizen will face potential incarceration that far exceeds his or her expected lifespan. For these and other reasons, citizens accused of crimes will often want to resolve their cases as quickly as possible by invoking their right to a speedy trial. But just how speedy is "speedy"? One month? Six months? Three years? As it turns out, the answer is "none of the above."

■ ■ ■

As a preliminary matter, it is important to distinguish between the many different kinds of speedy-trial rights. There is a speedy-trial right for federal cases, a speedy-trial right for interstate cases—that is, when the defendant is being held in custody in one state and charged criminally in another—and a speedy-trial right under the numerous state speedy-trial statutes as well. However, those speedy-trial rights either apply to relatively few of the total number of criminal cases, or don't offer much of a remedy to the defendant in the event they are violated. Consequently, the speedy-trial right we will discuss in this chapter is the constitutional right to a speedy a trial.

If a defendant's constitutional right to a speedy trial is violated, then the case must be dismissed with prejudice, which means that the case is dead and the state cannot file it again in the future. While this dismissal with prejudice is the ultimate remedy, it is also, for the most part, illusory. In reality, much like chasing the proverbial carrot on the stick, it is extremely difficult to obtain a dismissal with prejudice for the violation of the speedy-trial right. Why? Because just like the other constitutional rights, the right to a speedy trial is highly flexible, allowing the prosecutors and judges to bend it any which way they please.

A simple example will illustrate the malleable nature of this right. Assume that you are falsely accused of burglarizing your neighbor's garage, much like our hypothetical example in chapter 6, where we discussed the importance of cross-examination. You are arrested and are brought for your first court appearance the very next day, say, July 1, 2008. At that court appearance, commonly called the initial appearance, you receive a copy of the criminal complaint. (This is the formal charging document drafted by the prosecutor in order to commence the legal proceedings against you.) You also have your bond hearing, where the commissioner sets a fairly reasonable cash bail.

You are fortunate enough to have the resources to post the bail, and you are released from custody while your case is pending. During that time, however, you will also have to live under numerous bond conditions; but at least you're not decaying in jail while you wait for your trial date. Since you have the luxury of fighting your case "from the outside," you quickly find and hire a defense attorney. You and your attorney go to your preliminary hearing two weeks after your initial appearance, and then to your arraignment six weeks after that. At your arraignment, your attorney enters your "not guilty" plea and asks for a jury trial date, which the court sets for November 1, 2008.

At this point, you're thinking that four months from your initial appearance to jury trial really isn't that speedy. After all, they've got your cash that you posted for bail, you're living under restrictive bond conditions, and you've got the stress of the felony burglary charge hanging over your head—you're looking at a possible sentence of about a decade in prison if you're convicted. With this kind of all-consuming anxiety, it's not easy to function and get on with everyday life. You'd much prefer to get this done sooner, but you take what you can get. You and your attorney prepare for the November 1st trial date and subpoena all of your witnesses.

After months of stress, anxiety, and preparation, the big day finally arrives. You, your family, and your witnesses have taken off of work and are ready to defend the case. When you arrive in court on November 1st, however, you are surprised to learn that there are about a dozen other cases, all set for trial on the same day in front of the same judge. You also learn that many of the other cases are far older than yours, and many have already been passed over by the judge several times themselves. On top of that, many of the other defendants weren't able to post their cash bail, so they're still in custody and would therefore have priority over your case in the pecking order.

In light of all of this, the judge unapologetically gives you and your lawyer another trial date; your trial has been rescheduled for February 1st of the following year, 2009. The judge barks at you and your lawyer as though this delay was somehow your fault—after all, you didn't take a plea deal and instead demanded a jury trial—and informs you that your case will be high on his list of priorities for that day, so you'd better be ready to move forward with trial at that time. Your lawyer will, of course, prepare for trial once again, resubpoena your witnesses, and rack up additional attorney's fees along the way.

Months pass, and you go through the whole process once again, although both the trial preparation and your anxiety are a little easier this time around. When you arrive to court for jury trial on February 1st, however, the same thing happens again. This time, there are about ten other defendants ready for trial, and your case is still nowhere near the oldest of the cases. And because you have been fortunate enough to remain out of custody rather than in jail while your case is pending, you're still nowhere close to the top of the list when the judge decides which case has priority. Because the judge only holds one trial per week, he again puts your case off to a future date.

This time, however, before receiving your second postponed trial date (and third trial date overall), your lawyer demands a speedy trial on your behalf. This greatly upsets the judge. Many judges don't like it when defendants assert their rights and throw a monkey wrench into the already disorderly administration of justice. On top of that, this particular judge doesn't really understand the law regarding the constitutional right to a speedy trial.

This is obviously your lawyer's fault, so the judge is even more perturbed than usual. He therefore lashes out and attempts to punish your lawyer with a *really speedy* trial date, one that he thinks your lawyer won't be ready for: "Fine, you're going to trial *this Thursday*," the judge orders.

It turns out, however, that this tactic backfires on the judge. Your lawyer isn't at all afraid of going to trial, and her calendar just happens to be free this Thursday. "That's great, Judge, thanks," she responds. The prosecutor, however, frantically declares that *he* can't be ready that soon, as he's already released his witnesses from their subpoenas and just told them that trials are always on Mondays. The prosecutor then asks the judge for a later trial date. The ensuing dialogue goes like this:

Judge: All right, then, the new trial date will be April 15th.

Prosecutor: Fine by me, Judge.

Defense Lawyer: That doesn't work for me. I have two other trials on that day, scheduled in front of a different judge down the hall. I am free, however, each of the three weeks *before* and each of the three weeks *after* April 15th. Any of those dates would be great, Judge.

Judge: Well, Ms. Defense Lawyer, you just demanded a speedy trial and now you're turning down a trial date. Ms. Court Reporter, let the record reflect that Ms. Defense Lawyer is not available for the date that the court gave her for trial.

Defense Lawyer: Judge, will the record also reflect that I *was* available for the *first* date that you gave, but the prosecutor could not be ready, and that I *am* available for any of the six weeks *surrounding* the April 15th date?

Judge: No, it will not. Next available trial date is August 1st, and your client's right to a speedy trial is waived.

Defense Lawyer: Judge, you're confusing the statutory speedy-trial right with the constitutional speedy-trial right. The statutory right, even if waived, doesn't apply because my client is out of custody. We're talking about the constitutional right, and the difference is that . . .

Judge: Don't talk to me that way, Counsel! I've given you your trial date.

See how much fun that was? And, as it turns out, the real fun is just beginning. When your August 1st trial date finally rolls around, you, your lawyer, and your witnesses again show up, ready to go, but the prosecutor doesn't have all of his witnesses under subpoena and can't proceed to trial. He publicly complains about his workload and then requests yet another trial date. But this time you and your lawyer have had enough. After all, your case is now over one year old, you've formally asserted your right to a speedy trial, and yet it appears that you're nowhere near to actually *having* your constitutionally guaranteed speedy trial. So your lawyer moves to dismiss the case on the grounds that your right to a speedy trial was violated. You, of course, attach a reasonable and common meaning to the word "speedy" and are very confident that the judge will dismiss your case, despite his earlier in-court antics and apparent anger with you and your lawyer. Your reasonable expectations notwithstanding, however, you lose the motion to dismiss. It turns out that the delay in your case hasn't even come *close* to violating your speedy-trial right.

■ ■ ■

It is true that the constitutional speedy-trial right could be interpreted so that a defendant's trial must be started within a certain period of time—say, nine months or a year—unless the defendant waives the right or there is some compelling reason to go beyond the time limit. If this were the law, then the prosecutor would have to be a bit choosier about which cases he or she decided to prosecute in the first place; or, if the prosecutor wanted to continue with the current level of prosecutions in order to maintain the current crime rate in the community, he or she would have to make reasonable settlement offers to defendants so that fewer cases would go to trial. This would be a quick and reasonable way of dealing with the dozen or so cases, or even more, that are set for trial every Monday morning in each courtroom of the courthouse.

However, this would also be too simple and too certain, and would not be helpful in the "war" on whatever crime the government happens to be waging at any given time. Instead, when deciding whether a defendant's right to a speedy trial was violated, the judge will look at multiple factors, which can then be weighed and balanced in any manner the judge chooses. The factors that the judge must analyze are (1) the length of the delay; (2) the reasons for the delay; (3) whether the defendant formally asserted the speedy-trial right; and (4) the prejudice, if any, that the defendant suffered from the delay.[2]

For example, when deciding whether a defendant's right to a speedy trial has been violated, a delay of five years would weigh in the defendant's favor, whereas a delay of only eight months would favor the state. If the prosecutor was caught deliberately delaying the case in order to gain a tactical advantage, that factor—the *reason* for the delay—would weigh in the defendant's favor, whereas a delay for nearly any other reason would favor the state. If the defendant formally asserted his or her right by demanding a speedy trial, that factor would weigh in the defendant's favor, whereas a failure to make the demand early and often would favor the state. Finally, if the defendant had been unable to post bail and was in custody during the delay, the prejudice factor would favor the defendant, whereas if the defendant was out of custody during the delay, that factor would favor the state.

These examples, however, represent the clear-cut extremes at each end of the spectrum; but in reality, most facts don't fall so neatly onto one end or the other. Further, the four-factor speedy-trial balancing test looks and works very much like the other malleable constitutional rights that we covered in earlier chapters. In fact, you're probably already seeing several opportunities for the judge to rule against a defendant.

So how exactly would these four factors play out in your hypothetical burglary case that we discussed earlier in this chapter? First, your judge will look at the length of the delay. At the time that your attorney asked the court to dismiss your case, the delay was not that long: only thirteen months, or just over one year. The judge easily decides that this delay is not unusually long for his courtroom and, further, was not "shockingly long" by any standard.[3] Using this type of vague yet dramatic language allows the judge more flexibility than if he used a clear-cut numerical analysis. On top of that, the judge, having brushed up on the law since your last court appearance, points out that in many published court cases there have been delays of two years, three years, and even longer, and those delays did *not* violate the right to a speedy trial.[4] Measuring the length of the delay is only the first of the four factors, and you're already blown out of the water. But, for the sake of completeness—and for the pleasure of putting your lawyer in her place—the judge will analyze the remaining factors.

Second, the judge will determine the reason for the delay in your case. If you ever missed a court hearing, or if your lawyer ever had to reschedule a court hearing for any reason, the judge will seize on that in order to place blame for the delay on the defense, rather than on the government. (For the purpose of this analysis, both the prosecutor and the judge, appropriately so, are considered to be "the government," while you and your lawyer are considered to be "the defense.")

In your burglary case, however, you never missed a court date, and your attorney never had to reschedule any court hearing. But do you remember how your attorney was offered a trial date of April 15th but had to turn it down because of a conflict in her schedule? The judge will seize on that one instance and use it to blame the bulk of the delay on the defense. Never mind that your attorney accepted the first date that was offered by the judge, or that she *was* available for any of the six weeks surrounding the April 15th date. The judge now has another factor in the four-factor analysis to support his decision that your constitutional right to a speedy trial was not violated. And, further, the judge will decide that the other delays in your case—that is, the first two delays due to court congestion and the third delay due to the prosecutor's failure to subpoena his witnesses—were not intentional, and therefore should not be weighed heavily against the government.[5]

Third, the judge will determine whether you demanded a speedy trial, or were merely lying in the weeds, letting the time pass. In your case, the judge *has* to find that your lawyer demanded a speedy trial on your behalf; this was done in open court and on the record. However, your lawyer didn't demand it exactly when the judge would have liked, so this factor doesn't weigh in your favor either. In your case, your lawyer didn't make the demand until February 1st, and only after it was obvious that you would be facing a very lengthy delay. Even though there was no reason to demand a speedy trial before February 1st, her failure to make the demand at an earlier time weighs against the defense.

On top of that, even though the judge discourages speedy-trial demands, and attempts to not-so-subtly punish the defense lawyers who make them, the judge decides that your lawyer's demand was not made frequently enough or with enough fervor.[6] In other words, although your lawyer demanded a speedy trial, she should have done so earlier, more often, and more strenuously. Your lawyer's calm demeanor and professionalism, therefore, also weighs against you. And with the first three of four factors going against you, and in favor of the prosecutor, what initially looked like a strong defense motion now borders on the frivolous.

Fourth and finally, the judge will also determine whether you have been disadvantaged, or have suffered any prejudice, as a result of the delay. He decides, of course, that you have not. After all, you have been lucky enough to be out of custody, instead of sitting in jail while your case has been pending. But even if you were being held in jail, that still might not be enough unless you could show that your custody was somehow abnormally oppressive, whatever that means.[7] And, yes, the law says that your anxiety and concern over possibly being convicted *is* a form of prejudice, but the judge simply dismisses that as being typical of any criminal case, and not directly affecting your ability to defend against the allegation.[8]

In short, whatever you assert as being prejudicial, the judge will have an answer for it, or else he will find some way to turn the blame around on you or your lawyer. For example, a key defense witness moved out of state during the delay? You should have anticipated that and conducted a videotaped deposition before the witness left the state. Witnesses' recollections and memories have faded during the many years while the case was pending? Sorry, that's not specific enough to constitute prejudice.[9] Of course, if the witnesses knew specifically what they couldn't remember, their memories wouldn't be faded. This simple logic, however, is ignored in the judge's analysis.

Well, that's it. Those are the four prongs of the speedy-trial analysis, and you and your lawyer just had four swings and four misses. You came into court like a lion, and left like a lamb. And in some cases, it can get even worse. Even if you have three of the four factors in your favor, and only one of them weighs against you, the judge will simply attach more weight to that one factor and deny your motion. Or, worse yet, even if you have all four of the factors going in your favor, the judge can simply decide that the factors don't weigh heavily *enough* in your favor.

For example, even if your delay was well over two years, your defense lawyer just happened to have no other clients and therefore never had to turn down a trial date, you demanded your speedy trial early, often and with much bravado, and you suffered prejudice by being incarcerated while your case was pending, you could still lose your motion. How? There are many possible ways. Sure, two years is long, but not *too* long. Or incarceration is prejudicial, but your bail amount was reasonable, even though you didn't post it. Or the prejudice you claim—being incarcerated—didn't affect your ability to prepare for and defend your case. Or—and this is one of my very favorites—although the delay was the fault of the prosecutor, he was not delaying intentionally in order to gain an advantage at trial; rather, the delay was due to his negligence in not properly preparing his case. Therefore, the delay is weighed only minimally, rather than heavily, against the government.

Do you get an idea now of how this works? Simply stated, the constitutional right to a speedy trial has morphed into the government's right to file a criminal complaint, ensnare you in the criminal justice system, and then prosecute you at its leisure. All the while you'll risk losing valuable witnesses and testimony for your defense; you'll be under bond conditions or, worse yet, incarcerated pending trial; and you'll be living with the anxiety and fear of being locked up for years, for decades, or even for the rest of your life, depending on the charges you're facing. Sweet dreams.

■ ■ ■

Earlier in this chapter I naively suggested that this messy speedy-trial analysis could be fixed by interpreting the right "so that a defendant's trial must be started within a certain period of time—say, nine months or a year—unless the defendant waives the right or there is some compelling reason to go beyond the time limit." As it turns out, though, there are still ways to bypass such a rule, no matter how clear or clear-cut it seems to be. First, a phrase like "compelling reason" should set off alarm bells by now—remember how courts twisted the phrase "ongoing emergency" in chapter 6? And second, as the example below demonstrates, even fixed time periods are mere putty in the hands of prosecutors and judges.

There is actually a federal speedy-trial statute that is separate and distinct from the constitutional right to a speedy trial. That federal statute states that, for all cases to which it applies, a defendant's trial must begin within seventy days; however, that time can be extended for any delay in the case caused by motions. In one recent case, a defendant didn't get his trial within the seventy days, and the issue came down to whether the case was, in fact, "delayed" by three pretrial motions.[10] The defendant argued that the motions (two of which were filed by the prosecutor) didn't delay anything; in fact, the motions were either unopposed or quickly disposed of by the judge, and the trial date was never postponed because of them. So, the defendant's argument went, because the pretrial motions never caused any delay in the case, the seventy-day time period could not be extended, and the defendant's statutory right to a speedy trial was therefore violated.

Nice argument. However, the Supreme Court had a different view of things. It held that although the word *delay* "ordinarily indicates a postponement, it need not inevitably do so."[11] Instead, the Court believed, the word *delay* could be interpreted merely to measure "the interval between events"—in this case, the filing of the motions and their disposition.[12] In other words, sometimes these statutes require courts not to be so literal, but instead "to look at more general matters." And if that doesn't make sense, don't worry. The Court used a wonderful analogy that will make things crystal clear: "[A] statute that forbids the importation of 'wild birds' need not require a court to decide whether a particular parrot is, in fact, wild or domesticated. It may intend to place the entire species within that definition without investigation of the characteristics of an individual specimen."[13]

Yes, that clears things up nicely. But smoke, mirrors, and "wild birds" aside, the Court showed how shamelessly it can distort even a clear, simple statute mandating that a trial be held within a fixed number of days. In fact, as long as there are words involved—here, the seemingly clear and simple word *delay*—there will likely be judicial manipulation.

But don't worry about any of this speedy-trial business. Once you finally get to trial, you have the right to a fair trial in a fair tribunal, which includes a fair and impartial jury of your peers and an unbiased judge. We'll explore these constitutional rights in the next two chapters; surely, nothing could go wrong there.

NOTES

1. "In all criminal prosecutions, the accused shall enjoy the right to a speedy and public trial . . ." United States Constitution, Sixth Amendment, at www.law.cornell.edu/constitution/sixth_amendment (accessed November 5, 2011).

2. *Barker v. Wingo*, 407 U.S. 514 (1972).

3. For cases discussing the length of the delay, see *U.S. v. Schreane*, 331 F.3d 548 (6th Cir. 2003; delay not "shockingly long"); and *Doggett v. U.S.*, 505 U.S. 647 (1992; discussing length of delay in light of what is customary).

4. See, for example, *U.S. v. Serna-Villarreal*, 352 F.3d 225 (5th Cir. 2003).

5. For cases discussing the various reasons for the delay, and how the various reasons should be weighted against the parties, *see Barker v. Wingo*, 407 U.S. 514 (1972; discussing the difference between negligent delay and intentional delay); *U.S. v. Gregory*, 322 F.3d 1157 (9th Cir. 2003; same); and *U.S. v. Santiago-Becerril*, 130 F.3d 11 (1st Cir. 1997; delay to strengthen government's case not weighted against the government at all).

6. For cases discussing the manner in which the defendant asserts his or her right, see *Barker v. Wingo*, 407 U.S. 514 (1972; discussing the "frequency and force of the objections"); and *U.S. v. Grimmond*, 137 F.3d 823 (4th Cir. 1998; discussing the timing of the assertion of the right to a speedy trial).

7. *Hakeem v. Beyer*, 990 F.2d 750 (3rd Cir. 1993; mere incarceration not enough for prejudice; abnormally oppressive conditions of incarceration required).

8. *Klopfer v. N.C.*, 386 U.S. 213 (1967).

9. *U.S. v. Williams*, 372 F.3d 96 (2nd Cir. 2004; faded recollection and dim memories not specific enough to constitute prejudice).

10. *U.S. v. Tinklenberg*, 131 S.Ct. 2007 (2011).

11. Ibid.

12. Ibid.

13. Ibid.

Chapter Nine

A Fair and Impartial Jury of Your Peers?

In order for our system of justice to even have a chance of working, the accused citizen must be judged by a fair and impartial jury of peers. Why a jury? Because we citizens have, or at least should have, a healthy distrust of government, including the judiciary. And we want our jurors to be fair and impartial, of course, so that our fellow citizens' guilt or innocence is decided based on solid evidence and not bias, prejudice, assumptions, or preconceived notions. Further, the Constitution guarantees a fair and impartial jury to each and every one of us accused of a crime.[1]

When selecting a jury for a criminal trial, the typical procedure is to have a large group of potential jurors come into court. After questioning by the judge, the prosecutor, and the defense counsel, the pool is whittled down to twelve acceptable jurors plus one or more alternates, in the event that some jurors become ill or are otherwise unable to complete their service. This questioning process is known as voir dire—"to speak the truth"—and it is supposed to, at least in theory, weed out the jurors who are biased against the defendant.

Bias, of course, can take numerous forms.[2] One form, often called statutory bias, relates to the state legislature's having delineated certain things that automatically make a person biased and therefore ineligible to serve on a particular jury. For example, if a potential juror is related by blood or marriage to the prosecutor, that person is statutorily biased and, therefore, must be dismissed from the jury pool. Another form of bias, often called objective bias, is when other facts about the potential juror lead to the conclusion that no reasonable person in that position could be impartial. For example, if a potential juror were a lifelong friend of the prosecutor, and the two remained best friends at the time of trial, a person in that position would be under too much pressure to convict, and should be dismissed. Finally, the most easily understood form of bias is subjective bias. A potential juror is subjectively biased when, through his or her own words or actions during voir dire, the juror reveals an inability to be fair and impartial. Consider this hypothetical exchange, subtle variations of which frequently occur in voir dire:

Defense Counsel: Thank you all for coming today. The evidence will show that my client, the defendant, was in fact *arrested* by the police in this case. Does the fact that he was *arrested* make anyone think that he must be guilty of some crime?

Potential Juror #7: Yes. If the police arrested him, there was good reason.

Defense Counsel: Thank you for responding. Now, the judge told you earlier today that everyone charged with a crime is presumed innocent, and it is for you the jurors, and not the police or anyone else, to determine whether he is guilty. Do you still think that my client is guilty merely because he was arrested?

Potential Juror #7: Yes, if he was arrested, he did something wrong. That's just how I feel.

Defense Counsel: Do you think you could set that feeling aside, presume him innocent, and judge this case on the evidence?

Potential Juror #7. I'd really like to try, but I don't think I'd be fair. The police aren't going to waste their time with innocent people. I believe that the arrest alone shows that he's guilty.

Defense Counsel: But guilty of what? The judge hasn't yet read you the law or the elements of the crime with which he is charged. Why do you believe he must be guilty?

Potential Juror #7: I just do. I know a lot of police. They're good people.

Defense Counsel: Thank you very much for responding so honestly. That is the most important thing in this process, to get potential jurors to be honest about their beliefs and their views. *Your Honor, based on this juror's candor, I move that he be dismissed from the jury pool for subjective bias.*

This voir dire process, in theory, should work great, and should result in twelve unbiased jurors who are willing and able to judge the case based solely on the evidence presented in court. However, there are problems. The obvious and practical problem is that not every person will be as forthright as Potential Juror #7 was, above. The reality is that people can withhold their views and beliefs, or even outright lie about them, and most of the time no one will know the difference. However, there are bigger, more fundamental problems with voir dire. More specifically, judges are given such broad discretion that they often obstruct the process and keep it from working properly.

■ ■ ■

One judicial tactic that can obstruct the voir dire process is to dramatically limit the number and type of questions that defense counsel can ask potential jurors. And if a defense lawyer is not allowed to ask meaningful questions, then juror bias will never be discovered.

The way it works is this: Judges will begin voir dire with a series of their own questions. Many of these questions are so horribly phrased that they will never, under any circumstance, elicit a positive response. For example, imagine a large group of potential jurors, none of whom know each other, most of whom are terrified of speaking in public, and many of whom have never been in a courtroom before. All of this adds up to a highly uncomfortable situation, making it very unlikely that anyone will volunteer to answer even the most innocuous question. Then, with his first question out of the gate, the judge barks: "Does anyone here think the defendant is guilty because of his race or ethnicity?" Now, how many potential jurors, under these circumstances, will raise their hands and affirmatively answer that question? That's right: none. That question will never, ever elicit a positive response, and it is therefore useless.

Once the judge is done with his series of perfunctory and largely meaningless questions, the prosecutor gets his chance to ask questions; however, the prosecutor normally has no interest at all in knowing about racial biases, so he asks nothing further on that topic. Then it's the defense lawyer's turn. And, depending on the type of case and the client, the defense lawyer may have a deep interest in racial biases. But the defense lawyer knows better than to come out and essentially ask, much like the judge did, "Who among you is a racist?" That obviously won't work for two reasons: first, many people who are racially biased don't think of themselves as racially biased; and second, again, those who know they're racially biased certainly won't admit it in front of a judge and a roomful of strangers.

So instead, the defense lawyer would want to ask a series of questions like the following: Who among you has close friends of a race other than your own? What is the nature of your relationship? Who among you thinks inter-racial marriages could be difficult in today's society? Why do you think that? Do you think interracial marriage is a good or bad idea? Who among you works at a company that has an affirmative-action policy? There are conflict-ing views on affirmative action; what do you think about it?

These questions, unlike the judge's question which essentially asked for a public confession of racism, would reveal important facts about what people actually *do* and *believe*, rather than what they publicly *admit* that they do and believe. These questions could be incredibly useful in making educated deci-sions about which potential jurors may harbor some racial bias that would hurt the defendant's case. The problem, however, is that few judges would ever let a defense lawyer ask these questions. The prosecutor would object, and even if he didn't, the judge would jump in and stop the questioning immediately. Why? Because the judge already satisfied himself, as well as the court record for the possible appeal to follow, that none of the potential jurors are biased. How is he so sure? Because they impliedly said so by *not* raising their hands when the judge asked them, essentially, whether they're racist. Therefore, anything else on this topic is, in the judge's mind, repetitive and a waste of time.

How can judges get away with this? It's among the easiest things they'll do all day, actually. The law gives trial judges a tremendous amount of discretion in controlling their courtroom and the scope of the voir dire pro-cess. In nonlegal terms, this means they can do what they want and it's virtually unchallengeable on appeal. Granted, this particular judicial tactic is almost certainly motivated by a desire to get the trial started and over with, rather than to have racially biased jurors. In fact, it would no doubt be the rarest of judges who would actually desire a racially biased jury. However, regardless of the motivation, the end result is the same for the accused citi-zen: he or she will have a jury of randomly selected people who may know-ingly or unknowingly harbor significant and harmful racial biases.

■ ■ ■

Not all forms of bias are racial, of course. And with regard to nonracial biases, potential jurors are usually very forthright, especially when respond-ing to questions about their relationships with prosecutors or witnesses in the case, or about other nonsensitive topics. And once bias is uncovered—for example, when a potential juror reveals that he or she has a close relationship with the prosecutor—then the judge *has* to remove that person from the jury pool, right?

Although the judge should do so, there are two judicial tactics that some judges will use to avoid striking such jurors from the jury pool. One way that it's done is simply to decide, contrary to all of the evidence, that the juror is *not* biased. Here's a great example, taken from a published case.[3]

Defense Lawyer: Judge, I ask that you strike this potential juror for cause because she's an employee of the prosecutor's office.

Judge: What's the cause, Counselor?

Defense Lawyer: She's an employee of the prosecutor's office. She works for, and receives her paycheck from, the district attorney. The district attorney is prosecuting this case. She is objectively biased; that is, no reasonable person in her position could be impartial given where her bread is buttered, so to speak.

Judge: Is there authority for that?

Defense Lawyer: The authority is objective bias, Judge. I can't explain it any better.

Judge: I understand your *opinion*, but do you have any case-law authority for that?

Defense Lawyer: No, Judge. There was no way to anticipate this, so I didn't look up any cases before coming to court today. It's just common sense. It's so basic, there is no need for case law. She receives her paycheck from the office of the district attorney who is prosecuting this case. A reasonable person in that position could not be impartial.

Judge: Request to strike this juror is denied.

This example tells us a lot about trial judges. Why wouldn't the judge just be reasonable and err on the side of ensuring an impartial jury? Why wouldn't he just strike the biased juror from the pool, and avoid the lengthy and costly appeals process that would inevitably follow from this fiasco? Shouldn't an alarm bell have gone off in the trial judge's head, warning him that something just didn't feel right about this situation?

Instead, some trial judges, including this one, seem to look for any imaginable reason to keep the biased juror *in* the jury pool in order to benefit the prosecutor. Not only does this illustrate the judge's own bias in the case, but it also shows the great lengths to which some judges will go in order to ensure that defendants are convicted. The way in which the trial judge in the above example approached the issues—for example, by placing the burden of proof on the defense lawyer and by looking for any reason to keep the juror *in* the pool—speaks volumes of the judge's motivation.

This case also tells us a lot about appellate courts. Despite the three appellate judges who, to their credit, dissented—that is, they voted to overturn the defendant's conviction and give him a new trial with a fair and impartial jury—the majority of the appellate judges upheld the conviction. In so doing, they framed the issue in such a way as to put an incredible burden on the defense lawyer, rather than the judge or the prosecutor. They ultimately decided that because it was *possible* that a person employed by the prosecutor's office could have been impartial, the trial judge's decision not to remove the juror must be upheld.

Obviously, the way in which the issue is framed makes all of the difference in the world. The dissenting appellate judges, unlike the majority, decided quite reasonably, rationally, and cautiously that a juror's employer-employee relationship with the district attorney's office was simply unacceptable. The juror's loyalty to, and financial dependency on, the prosecutor was "so fraught with the possibility of bias that we must find objective bias regardless of the surrounding facts and circumstances and the particular juror's assurances of impartiality."[4] The juror, they believed, should never have been allowed to sit on the jury.

But was all of this really necessary? All anyone had to do was reverse the situation for a moment. Imagine that the defense lawyer's secretary, or even a secretary for another lawyer in his firm, was a potential juror. Imagine that the prosecutor then asked the judge to excuse that juror for objective bias. Does anyone seriously believe that the trial judge would have asked the prosecutor for case law to support the request before he removed the juror? Of course not. The defense lawyer's secretary would have been removed and reassigned to another trial in another court instantaneously.[5] What's good for the prosecutor should also be good for the defense. But that's not the case.

Other judges have allowed objectively biased individuals to remain on juries in other contexts as well. For example, some judges have refused to remove police officers from the jury, even though they were employed by the very same police department as the prosecutor's star witness.[6] One judge even refused to remove his own mother from the jury.[7] Why would this be a problem? Among other reasons, because the mother will obviously be biased toward her son, the judge. But, you might be thinking, the judge is neutral, so her bias wouldn't matter. Unfortunately, that possibility went out the window when the judge announced to the prospective jurors, including his mother, that he liked to consider himself "part of law enforcement."[8] The mother's pro-judge bias just shifted to pro-prosecutor and pro-police bias in a hurry.

Sensing this, the prosecutor opposed the defendant's motion to strike the judge's mother from the jury pool, and convinced the judge that his mother "had raised an individual (the judge) who looks at facts and tries to find the truth and that the judge's mother presumably would do the same as a juror."[9]

These few examples demonstrate that there are countless and creative ways in which judges can stack juries in favor of prosecutors just by deciding, contrary to the evidence, that objectively biased people are not biased. But what if the issue isn't one of objective bias, but instead subjective bias? What if a potential juror, much like Potential Juror #7 in our very first example, admits that he or she is biased, personally believes the defendant is guilty, and couldn't give the defendant a fair trial? In that case, where subjective bias has been established without a doubt, then the judge *must* strike the potential juror from the jury pool, right? Not even close. This situation only unleashes the judge's most potent weapon of all—one that is designed specifically for keeping subjectively biased jurors *in* the jury pool. It's called juror rehabilitation.

Let's pick up the example of Potential Juror #7 where we left off. Remember that Potential Juror #7 honestly answered that, because the defendant was at one point arrested by the police, he believed that he must be guilty. The potential juror was then challenged by the defense lawyer, but held firm that he believed the police and simply could not be fair and impartial. The defense lawyer then thanked the juror and asked the judge to remove him from the jury pool. Should the judge grant the defense lawyer's request? The juror clearly indicated that he could not be impartial, and believed the defendant was guilty. This is, after all, the precise definition of subjective bias. But this juror isn't even close to being removed, even though there are dozens of other jurors waiting in the wings to take his place. The judge, with his black robe, his command of the courtroom, and his position high on the bench—both figuratively and literally—could then use this position of authority to begin rehabilitating this juror. Here's how it works.

Defense Lawyer: Your Honor, based on his answers, I ask you to please strike Potential Juror #7 from the jury pool for subjective bias.

Judge: Not so fast, Counsel. Potential Juror #7, I am going to ask you some questions. Now, the law says that every person accused of a crime is innocent until proven guilty. Do you understand that?

Potential Juror #7: Yes.

Judge: And this defendant is only accused, and not yet convicted. Do you agree?

Potential Juror #7: Yes.

Judge: Therefore, he is presumed innocent, and you must view him that way unless the evidence proves otherwise, all right?

Potential Juror #7: If you say so.

Judge: No! It's not what *I* say. Well, it *is* what I say, but it also has to be what you believe. Now, do you understand and believe that?

Potential Juror #7: Yes, Judge. I'm sorry.

Judge: No! Don't be sorry. I want to know if *you* agree with what I said about the guilt or innocence of the defendant, and I want to know about *your* ability to presume him innocent. Now, do you agree with that, and can you do that?

Potential Juror #7: Um, yes?

Judge: Are you asking me or telling me?

Potential Juror #7: Telling. I'm telling you.

Judge: This juror is satisfactory and I will not strike him for subjective bias. Your motion to strike is denied. Now, do you have any more questions for the jury pool, Counsel?

Obviously, this is the worst thing a judge could do if his goal were really to select a fair and impartial jury. These questions will not ferret out the juror's true bias; that has already been done by defense counsel's questions. Instead, this course of questioning is designed to coerce the juror into accepting the judge's desired answer. Courts put a more attractive label on this practice— *rehabilitation* sounds much better than *coercion*, doesn't it? But we all know that it's impossible to change a person's lifelong views in five minutes, so this so-called rehabilitation is really nothing more than a superficial cover-up of the potential juror's bias. And it's an effective technique. How many people in the jury pool would publicly disagree with the stern and learned judge, in *his* courtroom no less? Few, if any, to be sure. The end result is that the potential juror is not removed for subjective bias and remains in the jury pool.

■ ■ ■

No discussion of a fair and impartial jury of one's peers would be complete without reference to *Batson v. Kentucky*.[10] This case comes into play during the second part of jury selection, after the biased jurors have been removed—or not removed, as the case may be—from the jury pool. At that point, both the prosecutor and the defense lawyer are allowed a handful of peremptory strikes wherein they can remove from the jury pool any remaining juror for any reason they wish—except for purely discriminatory reasons such as race. If the defense lawyer suspects the prosecutor is violating this antidiscrimination rule by striking potential jurors because of their race, he or she can raise a *Batson* challenge.

Here's how it works: Suppose you are a defense lawyer, and you are defending a client who is accused of resisting a police officer. Your client is a member of a minority group, and your defense is that he didn't resist, but rather was targeted by police because of his race. After the first part of jury selection where the biased participants have been weeded out for cause, you and your client are pleased that there are five remaining potential jurors who are also members of your client's minority group. This commonality of background and life experiences—including possible experiences in dealing with police—will be critical in a case like this. You and your client are pleased to have a true jury of his peers.

At this point, then, the pool has a total of twenty-three potential jurors, and each side will now exercise its five peremptory strikes. This will whittle the pool down to thirteen jurors—the twelve that are needed plus one alternate. You strike one juror because he first indicated that he thought your client was guilty, but was then rehabilitated by the judge and left in the pool, despite your objection. You strike another juror because his brother is a police officer on the local police department; the judge wouldn't remove him for cause either, but you'll wipe him out with a peremptory strike.

You complete your strikes in this manner. Then, when the judge names the jurors who have been selected for service and asks them to stand up, you notice that all the potential jurors who are members of your client's minority group remain seated. These citizens will *not* be in the jury because the prosecutor exercised his five peremptory strikes to eliminate them all. Your client now has no minorities in his jury; it is no longer a jury of his peers. But you remember the case of *Batson v. Kentucky* and quickly raise a *Batson* challenge, which requires the prosecutor to give a race-neutral explanation for striking the minority participants.

As you might have guessed, providing a race-neutral reason to justify striking a minority juror is incredibly easy. You will likely lose your challenge, and your client will have his fate decided by a jury without a single minority member. What kind of race-neutral reasons might the prosecutor successfully offer? Any, really. In fact, the law holds that the reason the prosecutor chooses to offer "does not have to be persuasive or even plausible."[11] Your judge will accept "even a silly or superstitious reason, if facially nondiscriminatory."[12] That's right, implausible, silly, and superstitious reasons are welcome, and are good enough to justify removing minority members from your minority client's jury pool.

Here, then, are some race-neutral justifications that have been *accepted* by the courts, and which your particular prosecutor is likely to use. The prosecutor might say that he didn't strike the potential juror because of race, but rather because of his hair or facial hair.[13] Or because she was too young.[14] Or because he had strong religious beliefs.[15] Or because she was a social worker.[16] Or because he served on a previous jury where that defendant was acquitted.[17] Or because she seemed grandmotherly.[18] Or because the prosecutor was looking for a jury of "average, typical, born-and-bred" local residents, and the stricken minority juror just didn't fit the bill.[19] And usually, these reasons will be accepted even when they would have applied equally to White jurors whom the prosecutor left on the jury.[20]

These examples lead to the obvious question: Have any stated reasons for striking minority jurors ever been *rejected* by the courts? Yes, actually. Sometimes the reasons aren't really reasons at all. If the prosecutor strikes a minority juror and can only say that he or she did so based on intuition or a hunch, this so-called reason might not be specific enough.[21] Or if the prosecutor offers a reason that is clearly contradicted by the record—for example, justifying removal of a minority juror for being too religious when, in fact, the juror said during voir dire that he was an atheist—this might also be rejected.[22]

Finally, one prosecutor, who was either particularly inept *or* especially unethical but honest—a curious combination of traits—admitted that he struck a juror mainly because he was "a Black man with no kids and no family."[23] After the *Batson* challenge was raised, this should have been a slam-dunk decision for the judge: clearly, "Black man" is not a race-neutral explanation, and the prosecutor should not have been allowed to strike that potential juror. Alarmingly, however, the trial judge *accepted* "Black man" as a race-*neutral* explanation. And when the defendant appealed his conviction, the state had the nerve to argue that the prosecutor—despite having said that the juror's skin color "was one of the main things I have a problem with"—was merely being "descriptive" when identifying the juror to the court.[24] Fortunately, although it took many years of costly litigation, a higher court decided that the trial judge botched the call, and reversed the defendant's conviction.

■ ■ ■

You can now see that we haven't even begun the evidence portion of the trial, and things are already stacked against the accused. The bad news is that things could get worse. Now that the jury has been selected, let's take a closer look at the role of the judge and the prosecutor, which we'll cover in the next two chapters.

NOTES

1. In all criminal prosecutions, "the accused shall enjoy the right to . . . trial, by an impartial jury of the state and district wherein the crime shall have been committed . . ." United States Constitution, Sixth Amendment, at http://www.law.cornell.edu/constitution/sixth_amendment (November 5, 2011).

2. For a case discussing the three different types of juror bias that are explained in this chapter, see *State v. Smith*, 2006 WI 74.

3. *State v. Smith*.

4. Ibid.

5. In a case that more closely parallels the case of the prosecutor's employee being on the jury, one judge discovered, four days into a trial, that a sitting juror's children had previously been prosecuted by a different prosecutor in the prosecutor's office. And even though the judge admitted there was no basis to remove her for cause, especially not midtrial, he did just that. The juror was removed and sent home. *State v. Czysz*, 2010AP2804-CR (Wis. Ct. App. 2011).

6. *State v. Louis*, 457 N.W.2d 484 (Wis. 1990).

7. *State v. Tody*, 2009 WI 31.

8. Ibid.

9. Ibid.

10. *Batson v. Kentucky*, 476 U.S. 79 (1986).

11. *State v. Marquez*, 2011 WI App 58.

12. *State v. Lamon*, 2003 WI 78, ¶31.

13. *Purkett v. Elem*, 514 U.S. 765 (1995).

14. *DeBerry v. Portuondo*, 403 F.3d 57 (2nd Cir. 2005).

15. *U.S. v. DeJesus*, 347 F.3d 500 (3d Cir. 2003).

16. *U.S. v. Meza-Gonzales*, 394 F.3d 587 (8th Cir. 2005).

17. *U.S. v. George*, 363 F.3d 666 (7th Cir. 2004).

18. *Boyde v. Brown*, 404 F.3d 1159 (9th Cir. 2005).

19. *U.S. v. Spriggs*, 102 F.3d 1245, 1254 (D.C. Cir. 1996).

20. *State v. Marquez*.

21. *Hardcastle v. Horn*, 368 F.3d 246 (3rd Cir. 2004).

22. For the general proposition that the reason given cannot be contrary to the objective facts, see *McClain v. Prunty*, 217 F.3d 1209 (9th Cir. 2000).

23. *Walker v. Girdich*, 410 F.3d 120 (2nd Cir. 2005).

24. Ibid.

Chapter Ten

Judicial Bias

A Fair Trial in a Fair Tribunal?

In order for citizens to have any level of confidence in a system of criminal justice, and in order for a defendant to receive a fair trial, an unbiased judge is an absolute necessity. This right to a "fair trial in a fair tribunal" is guaranteed to all by our constitutional right to due process. [1]

Why is an unbiased judge so important when it is the jury, and not the judge, that decides the outcome of a criminal case? It is true that unless the defendant waives the right to a jury trial, it is the jury, and not the judge, that returns the verdict of guilty or not guilty. (The judge must then enter a judgment that should be consistent with that verdict, but sometimes the judge will get it wrong—for example, by entering a judgment of guilt on a not-guilty verdict—and will need to be corrected.) However, the judge still has a tremendous influence on the outcome of every case. The judge will often, either consciously or subconsciously, greatly impact a defendant's trial and, in some cases, can all but ensure a guilty verdict.

More specifically, as we saw in chapters 4 and 5, it is the judge who decides what evidence—both in terms of testimony and physical evidence—the state will be allowed to use against a defendant. As we saw in chapter 6, it is the judge who decides which of the state's witnesses and accusations the defendant will be permitted to confront, or cross-examine, at trial. As we saw in chapter 9, it is the judge who decides which jurors are allowed to remain in the jury pool, and which are dismissed because they are biased against the defendant. And as we will see in chapter 11, it is the judge who decides which trial tactics, no matter how improper, the prosecutor will be allowed to get away with.

Finally, the judge will also decide numerous other important issues throughout the course of a trial—for example, what questions defense counsel can ask on cross-examination, what evidence the defendant can present to the jury, and what instructions the judge will give to the jury—all of which will have a direct and substantial impact on the jury's ultimate verdict. Consequently, a fair trial—not only in actual fairness but also in the appearance of fairness—is virtually impossible if the judge has an opinion that the defendant is guilty, or in any way favors the prosecutor.

Unfortunately, despite the tremendous importance of an unbiased judge, the reality is that trial judges are allowed to do, say, and get away with things that would get anyone else in any other profession fired on the spot. First, judges have the power to completely disregard the law, and they suffer no penalty or repercussion for doing so. Much like with the reckless filing of baseless criminal complaints by the prosecutor, the judge is not accountable to anyone for the life-ruining consequences of his or her reckless, or even intentionally bad, judicial rulings. When a trial judge knowingly rules contrary to the law in order to obtain the result that he or she wants, the defendant may have to spend years in prison hoping that an appellate court will some day correct the error and remand the case for new trial.

Second, and more to the point of this chapter, some judges do not even *try* to appear neutral in the cases over which they preside. Judicial behavior, by some judges in some cases, ranges from fairly mild forms of disgust—such as incessant sighing and repeated eye rolling in front of the jury when the defendant is presenting evidence—to highly prejudicial rulings against defendants, and even verbal abuse of defense counsel in front of the jury. But instead of correcting these judicial abuses, our system merely puts a Band-Aid on the problem. Near the end of the trial, the judge will usually read a standard instruction to the jury, stating something like this: "If any member of the jury has an impression of my opinion as to whether the defendant is guilty or not guilty, disregard that impression entirely and decide the issues of fact solely as you view the evidence."[2] This insulting instruction—which is not only completely ineffective but actually reminds the jury of the judge's disdain for the defendant—is assumed to cure any appearance of bias and will defeat most subsequent claims that the defendant's constitutional right to a fair tribunal was violated.

Once again, despite the incredible importance of an unbiased judge, this constitutional right is a soft law. There are no basic, firm rules about what a trial judge may and may not do, or how the judge must conduct him- or herself in front of the jury. This, of course, would be too much like the basic workplace structure and rules under which the rest of us must operate on a daily basis. Instead, when reviewing misconduct by trial judges, appellate judges often minimize the wrongdoing with pompous, linguistic dances, and create excuses or even justifications for the trial judge's behavior. All of this, of course, is done on their way to deciding that the defendant was simply unable to prove judicial bias, and therefore the constitutional right to a fair tribunal was not violated.

■ ■ ■

Judicial bias manifests itself in many forms. One form is when the judge harshly criticizes the defense lawyer in front of the jury, during the trial. For example, a trial judge, already frustrated that a defendant has taken up so much of his time by demanding a trial instead of merely pleading guilty, may not like the defense lawyer's style, methods, or questions during cross-examination. The judge may then openly criticize the defense lawyer, which not only gives the jury the impression that the judge is on the prosecutor's side, but could also adversely affect the defense lawyer's presentation for the remainder of the case.[3]

When reviewing claims of this type of bias, however, appellate courts refuse to criticize the trial judge or find that the judge violated any rule of trial decorum. Instead, they will minimize the judge's behavior by characterizing it, for example, as merely undeserving "of inclusion in a trial advocacy textbook."[4] That is, even though the judge's treatment of defense counsel in front of the jury "could have been a bit more measured," the appellate court will simply conclude that the defendant was unable to prove actual prejudice.[5] Then the appellate court's desired conclusion—that the defendant's right to a fair tribunal was *not* violated—naturally follows. And on what does the appellate court base this decision? Not much of anything, actually, other than its desire to affirm the defendant's conviction and save the trial judge from some much-deserved criticism and a retrial.

Another form of judicial bias occurs when the case is not going very well for the prosecutor, and the judge simply interrupts the trial, steps in, and takes over questioning.[6] The judge is free to do this, even though ours is an *adversarial* system of justice where both the state and the defendant are represented by an attorney, and the judge is supposed to be neutral and unbiased. For example, if a defense lawyer is having some success cross-examining a state's witness by impeaching him with his prior, inconsistent statements, the judge can simply stop the action, step in, and rehabilitate the witness. The judge can do this by offering the witness a potential explanation for his inconsistency, or he may even instruct the jury that he, the judge, didn't view the witness's testimony as being inconsistent at all.

When reviewing this type of bias, an appellate court will often conclude—just as they do in cases where the trial judge criticizes the defense lawyer in front of the jury—that although "the content of [the judge's] statements might be seen as favoring the prosecution," that is not enough to "make them so prejudicial that a reversal is warranted."[7] Again, on what is this determination based? Remember, the right to a fair and impartial trial judge is a soft law, so the answer is *nothing*. Nothing, that is, other than the appellate court's desire to preserve the conviction, spare the trial judge any embarrassment, and avoid a retrial.

■ ■ ■

Although we have introduced the topic of judicial misbehavior, the forms of bias discussed thus far—even though highly damaging to a defense lawyer's ability to do his or her job, and highly prejudicial to the defendant—have been, relatively speaking, quite mild. As it turns out, trial judges are actually entitled to commit far greater misconduct before an appellate court will decide that they violated a defendant's right to a fair tribunal.

Consider the case of *Bracy v. Schomig*, where the defendant appealed his conviction and subsequent death sentence.[8] The basis for his appeal was that his trial judge had been taking cash bribes from rich defendants in *other* cases, during the same time as this defendant's case. This bribe taking created the very real possibility that the judge was unfair to nonbribing defendants. The motivation to be unfair to them, of course, would be to compensate for the appearance that he was being soft on crime or prodefendant with the rich, bribe-paying defendants. Given this, it would seem reasonable that a nonbribing defendant—if convicted at trial in front of this judge during the time period when the judge was accepting bribes from other defendants—should get a new trial in a fair tribunal. You might even assume that, under these extreme circumstances, ordering a new trial would be a slam-dunk decision, right? Well, you'd be wrong. Even with a crooked, bribe-taking judge, and even when the judge repeatedly ruled in favor of the prosecutor on key issues throughout the case, all this was still not enough to find that the judge was biased. Why not? Because the appellate court put the burden of proof on the defendant, and simply held that the defendant couldn't *prove* actual bias, no matter how bad things looked on the surface.

In this case the appellate court pointed out—quite accurately, in fact—that it is quite common for judges to repeatedly rule in favor of the prosecutor on evidentiary issues and other trial-related matters. (See the last part of chapter 7 for a more detailed discussion of how this works.) Therefore, the appellate court just couldn't bring itself to assume that the bribe-taking judge was, in fact, biased in this particular case. That is, all of the judge's proprosecution rulings looked pretty much like every other case in every other court.

The appellate court did, however, reverse the death sentence that had been delivered after the trial and conviction. In other words, the court affirmed the conviction, but held that "it is a fair, if not inevitable, inference that [the judge] used the death penalty hearing to deflect suspicion that might be aroused because of, say, his acquittal of another accused murderer who had bribed him."[9]

Why was it proper to reverse the defendant's death sentence, but not the conviction that led to the sentence? Both the conviction and the sentence occurred in the same judge's court, and during the time that judge was taking bribes from other defendants in other cases. As one group of dissenting judges on the appellate court pointed out: "There is no basis for supposing [the judge] *unbiased* until the defendant [was] convicted, then *biased* at the sentencing hearing."[10] But before you think these dissenters were a bastion of fairness on the court, know this: they didn't vote to reverse the conviction and the death sentence; instead, they voted to uphold them both. At least they were consistent.

In reality, of course, both the majority and this group of dissenters on the appellate court completely missed the point. First, based on the facts in the case, the bribe-taking judge was obviously biased during the sentencing hearing. For example, his remarks were incredibly pro-prosecutor, and his rulings were made "without any articulated reasons."[11] He even tried to discourage the defendant's lawyer "from making a closing argument when the jury's choice of penalty was between life and death."[12] Second, the bribe-taking judge would never have been able to get to the sentencing hearing if he hadn't first ensured that the defendant was convicted. In reality, therefore, the inference of bias must run not only to the sentencing hearing, but also to the underlying trial and conviction, without which there wouldn't have been a sentencing hearing.

As a *second* group of dissenters on the court observed, the decision to affirm the conviction was probably—and somewhat ironically, considering that this case revolved around bribery—motivated by economics. In other words, this crooked judge "presided over the disposition of thousands of cases, and recognizing his lack of impartiality in one case presents the prospect that all of the cases he handled must be vacated. Indeed, that uncomfortable prospect is the one and only justification that has been offered over the long history of this litigation for concluding that a thoroughly corrupt judge amounts to a constitutionally acceptable decision-maker."[13]

To their credit, this second group of dissenters voted to reverse not only the death penalty, but also the underlying conviction, stating that "[d]ue process means something, and in [our] view it means something more than trial and the infliction of the ultimate punishment before the likes of a judicial racketeer."[14] Unfortunately, however, this group of dissenters wasn't persuasive enough to convince their fellow judges to give the defendant a new trial.

■ ■ ■

As alarming as the previous section (hopefully) is, forget, for a moment, about this business of *inferences* of bias. What if a judge comes out and actually says that he believes you are guilty, long before your trial and any conviction? Is that enough to prove that the judge is biased and to get you a new trial in a fair tribunal? Don't bet on it.

Assume that you are charged with a crime—say, disorderly conduct against your spouse—and that you are released on bail before your trial date. While out on bail, you are accused of committing a second crime—say, having a phone conversation with your spouse, in violation of a bond condition that prohibits contact. The cases are consolidated into one trial; but before your trial date, the judge has another, unrelated case where *that* defendant has asked to be released on bail. The judge says no to that defendant, and sets forth his reasons in a memorandum. In so doing, he also expresses his opinion on bail generally, and specifically states that it shouldn't be granted in certain circumstances. To support this view, he references your pending cases and uses *you* as an example of how defendants violate bond conditions when they are released on bail. He is assuming that you are guilty of at least one, and probably both, of the allegations against you, long before you've even had your trial.

Your lawyer finds out about the judge's written discussion of you and your cases in the other, unrelated case. Your lawyer believes, and for good reason, that the judge has already decided your guilt and is biased against you. He therefore asks the judge to step down in your case. The legal issues are captured in this exchange.[15]

> **Your Attorney**: Judge, my client is only *alleged* to have committed a second crime while released on bail. He has not yet been tried and is presumed innocent of all allegations. He is entitled to an unbiased judge who has not formed an opinion that he is guilty. The memorandum that you wrote in your *other* case, however, proves that you believe my client is guilty in *this* case. Please step down from this case, and have a different judge assigned.

> **Judge**: I am not biased against your client. End of story.

Your Attorney: Judge, I know you're *saying* you're not biased, but the evidence shows that you are biased. Your memorandum in the other case says that defendants do bad things when they're released on bail. To support that claim, you wrote about how my client committed a crime while he was out on bail.

Judge: I referred to your client's crime as an "alleged crime," if you would take the time to read it closely, Counsel.

Your Attorney: Judge, you can't put the magic word *alleged* in front of the word *crime* and expect that it will cure the bias. You obviously believe my client committed the crime while on bail. If you *didn't* believe that, you wouldn't have used his case as an example of how defendants do bad things when they're out on bail.

Judge: Counsel, I am not biased, and I will not step down from this case. I have heard quite enough.

Can you guess what happened? If you were this defendant, the judge stayed on the case and presided over your jury trial. And, unfortunately for you, you were convicted of all charges. You then appealed to the state appellate court, arguing that your trial judge was biased because he prejudged your guilt before trial. But the state appellate court decided that because the judge *said* he was not biased, and because he used the word *alleged* when describing your crimes in his memorandum in the other case, he was, in fact, not biased. [16] Your conviction stands.

Ten years later, however, after multiple appeals and many thousands of dollars in taxpayers' money, a federal court pointed out the folly of the state appellate court's reasoning. [17] The federal court understood what your lawyer was saying a decade earlier when he politely asked the judge to recuse himself from your case. That is, the trial judge had already made up his mind, before your trial, that you were guilty; otherwise, he wouldn't have cited your case to support his opinion that defendants do bad things while released on bail. Sprinkling the word *alleged* into his memorandum just wasn't enough to change that. [18]

Despite this anomalous outcome—where relief from judicial bias was, in a sense, obtained, albeit ten years too late—the fact is that appellate courts have saddled defendants with an unreasonable and impossibly high burden in proving that judges are *not* fair and impartial. Instead of demanding appropriate, professional behavior from judges in the courtroom—which is nothing more than demanding that they do the job for which they receive a handsome government salary and benefits—the appellate courts usually coddle them and look for any justification, no matter how intellectually weak, to uphold even the most biased and harmful judicial behavior.

In fact, as we have seen, to prove judicial bias it is not enough to merely show that there was improper judicial conduct that favored the government. In addition to that, the defendant must also prove to the appellate court that the judge's misconduct caused him or her "serious prejudice."[19] Of course, this is usually an impossible task—even when there is a "a tag-team effect between the judge and prosecution that could not have been lost on the jury"[20]—because the legal standard is deliberately designed to prevent the defendant from winning an appeal.

In other words, how can a defendant possibly prove that it was the judge's misconduct, and not something else that occurred during his week- or month-long trial, that hurt his case? And even if he could, how could he prove that it *seriously* hurt his case? These soft and malleable words do nothing more than create wiggle room for the appellate court to decide that while the judge may have acted improperly, he was not legally biased, and therefore the defendant's conviction must stand. On top of all of that, the defendant must meet his heavy burden based solely on the cold record—that is, the typed transcript consisting only of printed words—without any ability for the appellate court to see, hear, or feel the impact of the judge's misconduct on the jury. Good luck with that.

Chapter 4 demonstrated how ridiculous the law can be by applying the logic of a rule to a different, real-world setting. Let's do the same here. Imagine the disastrous results we would have if other professionals could get away with the type of behavior that trial judges often get away with. Imagine an engineer, before designing a bridge, throwing away the engineering textbook in order to build the bridge however he pleased, ignoring all repercussions. Imagine a doctor making medical decisions based on what suited her, rather than what was best for her patients. Imagine a court reporter transcribing what he believed the lawyer should have said or meant to say, rather than what she actually said. The examples are limited only by our imagination. Even filmmakers and writers—who are among the most creative and free-flowing people among us—are constrained to great degree by structure and convention. To date, however, no such rules, laws, or general principles have been able to effectively reign in the rogue judges of our judiciary.

■ ■ ■

There are no doubt judges who are fair and impartial, and who are also very smart and make honest efforts to apply the law as it is, rather than as they think it should be. And there are even judges who aren't concerned in the least if their decisions upset the prosecutor or the police, or work to the disadvantage of the government. I have even practiced in front of some judges like this. But this chapter isn't about praising the judges who do their jobs. They are already rewarded with excellent compensation and, more importantly, the trust of the public.

And that is the precise point that some other judges need to understand. No judge—whether elected or appointed—is on the bench because he or she has the right to be there. Rather, judges are there because they have been entrusted to serve the citizenry. And no judge is there to prejudge the defendant or help the prosecutor win a case. Rather, judges are there to uphold the Constitution, "to conduct fair proceedings," and to protect "the rights of even the most [apparently] undeserving defendants."[21] That is, to provide a "fair trial in a fair tribunal."[22]

NOTES

1. For the right to a "fair trial in a fair tribunal" see *Bracy v. Gramley*, 520 U.S. 899 (1997). See also United States Constitution, Fourteenth Amendment, at www.law.cornell.edu/constitution/amendmentxiv (accessed November 12, 2011), which states that "No state shall . . . deny to any person within its jurisdiction the equal protection of the laws."
2. This language was taken from Wisconsin Jury Instruction Criminal 100.
3. *U.S. v. Mohammad*, 53 F.3d 1426 (7th Cir. 1995).
4. Ibid.
5. Ibid.
6. *U.S. v. Verser*, 916 F.2d 1268 (7th Cir. 1990).
7. Ibid.
8. *Bracy v. Schomig*, 286 F.3d 406 (7th Cir. 2002).
9. Ibid.
10. Ibid.
11. Ibid.
12. Ibid.
13. Ibid.
14. Ibid.
15. This hypothetical case and dialogue are based on *State v. Franklin*, 1998 Wisc. App. Lexis 480.
16. Ibid.
17. *Franklin v. McCaughtry*, 398 F.3d 955 (7th Cir. 2005).
18. Ibid.
19. *U.S. v. Washington*, 417 F.3d 780 (7th Cir. 2005).
20. Ibid.
21. *Bracy v. Schomig.*
22. *Bracy v. Gramley.*

Chapter Eleven

Prosecutor Misconduct and the "Harmless Error"

When two tennis greats step onto the court for a championship match, they must play by a set of rules. When two martial artists climb into the octagon for a cage fight, they must fight by a set of rules. When two chess champions square off against each other, you guessed it: rules. And even when two nations engage in something as brutal as war, rules will apply. In fact, nearly all adversarial or competitive endeavors—whether intellectual, brutal, or both—have rules. This is not only necessary but desirable. The same is true, of course, of the criminal jury trial. When a prosecutor files charges and the defendant denies the allegations and demands a trial, there are rules that govern the conduct of the lawyers—at least in theory.[1]

The constitutional right to due process, along with other constitutional provisions, statutes, and rules of procedure, combine to form the rules of the game for criminal trials. Some of these rules even apply before, and in anticipation of, the trial. For example, within a reasonable time before trial the prosecutor must disclose to the defendant all exculpatory evidence—that is, evidence that tends to prove a defendant's innocence—so that the defendant may use it at trial.[2] (This type of evidence includes DNA or other scientific tests that eliminate the defendant as a suspect, as well as eyewitness statements claiming that someone other than the defendant committed the crime.) Another example of a pretrial rule, and one that we saw in chapter 9, is that when selecting the jury in voir dire the prosecutor may not peremptorily strike potential jurors simply because they are the same race or ethnicity as the defendant.[3]

These rules of the game, of course, are just as important during the actual trial. When cross-examining a witness the prosecutor may not ask questions about inadmissible or irrelevant facts, or imply to the jury, through his questions of the witness, that he secretly knows the defendant is guilty.[4] Also during the course of a trial (but outside of the courtroom), the prosecutor may not intimidate or otherwise influence witnesses in order to make them change their testimony to help the state's case.[5] For example, the prosecutor may not give government witnesses gifts—drugs, cash, clothing, or any one of numerous other amenities—in exchange for testimony, especially without disclosing these favors to defense counsel.[6] Similarly, the prosecutor may not arrange for paralegals to have phone sex with incarcerated government "snitch-witnesses"—again, at least not without disclosing these extraordinary favors to defense counsel, who may then use them to demonstrate the witness's progovernment bias at trial.[7] (And yes, these things have really happened.)

Near the end of the trial, in closing arguments to the jury, the prosecutor is only permitted to argue about the actual evidence that was presented at trial.[8] For example, he may not abuse his closing argument by testifying about his own personal beliefs or vouching for the credibility of the government's witnesses.[9] (This "no vouching" rule even applies, and is especially important, when the prosecutor liked the witness enough to give him or her cash, phone sex, and other gifts in exchange for testimony.) Likewise, the prosecutor may not attempt to improperly sway or intimidate the jury into reaching a verdict of guilt by appealing to their racial biases or prejudices.[10] Similarly, he may not argue to the jury that the defendant *must* be guilty because he or she exercised one or more constitutional rights, such as the right to remain silent at trial.[11]

And just as most crime goes undetected, so too does most prosecutorial misconduct, especially when it occurs before trial, or even during trial but outside of the courtroom. But considering only the misconduct that we know about, the problem is still widespread. On one end of the spectrum, this misconduct includes acts that are often dismissed as mere negligence, such as "forgetting" to turn over exculpatory evidence. On the other end of the spectrum is misconduct that would be categorized as intentional, such as bribing witnesses, fabricating evidence of guilt, and consciously withholding exculpatory evidence.

The poster child for intentional prosecutor misconduct would have to be the prosecutor in the infamous Duke lacrosse scandal.[12] He both suppressed and falsified evidence to prosecute obviously innocent college students for his own political gain in an upcoming election. Fortunately, though, good defense lawyers defend their clients vigorously despite the public outcry in support of "the victim," and even in the face of what (at first) appears to be overwhelming evidence of guilt. In the end, thanks to the Duke lacrosse players' defense lawyers, the prosecutor's misconduct was discovered and exposed.

Although the Duke lacrosse players got justice, and the prosecutor was eventually removed from his political office and even disbarred, this is a rare outcome. In fact, prosecutorial misconduct, even when detected, is usually ignored. One elected district attorney, for example, was "admonished . . . for two failures to disclose discoverable material" to defense counsel.[13] What does "admonished" mean? In this case, it meant that the appellate court acknowledged that the prosecutor's behavior was "inexcusable," but then ruled for the government anyway.[14] Then, when a different defendant appealed his conviction because the same prosecutor withheld evidence in his case, the appellate court again acknowledged the prosecutorial misconduct, but again ruled for the government.[15] And even after all of this, and one other known instance of misconduct, the prosecutor merely got a "public reprimand."[16] And what good did the "admonishment" and the "public reprimand" do? Not much. The prosecutor was later reelected as district attorney.[17]

These particular prosecutorial antics aside, however, the policy behind the rules of criminal procedure is clear. We don't want a jury to convict a defendant because a prosecutor purposely hid, or even merely "forgot" to turn over, evidence; rather, we want the jury to reach its verdict based on all of the relevant evidence.[18] We don't want a jury to convict a defendant because a prosecutor influenced witnesses through gifts and extraordinary favors; rather, we want the jury to reach its verdict based on truthful and accurate testimony. And we don't want the jury to convict a defendant because a prosecutor was good at whipping up the deep-seated racial biases of the jurors; rather, we want the jury to reach its verdict based on evidence, and not on passion or prejudice. As these limited examples show, strict adherence to the procedural rules of the game is incredibly important, not only to the individual citizen who is accused of the crime, but also to society and the criminal justice system more generally.

■ ■ ■

The importance of enforcing the rules of the game is a point better made with an analogy—an analogy that has been explicitly adopted by the U.S. Supreme Court. Suppose that you're a boxer, and you're training for a title fight. In boxing, of course, there are well-established and familiar rules that you and your opponent must follow. Much the same as criminal law, some of these rules apply before you even set foot in the ring. For example, when training for your fight, you cannot use steroids. You will also have to watch your weight, keeping it under a certain limit so that you and your opponent will fall into the same weight class, thereby making it a fair fight. And when you step into the ring to actually fight your opponent, the action will be governed by numerous additional rules. For example, you'll only be allowed to throw punches above the belt. And you won't be allowed to use your elbows or forearms to strike your opponent; rather, only your gloved fists may be used for striking.

These rules of the boxing game, much like the rules that govern a criminal jury trial, are simple and straightforward. They are also well-known, especially to the referee, the participants, and the serious fan, if not to the general public or the casual observer. These rules are not vague or secretive; rather, they are purposefully clear and easy to follow. Given this, you will incorporate all of these rules into your prefight regimen. You will design a nutrition program, without steroids, that will keep you under the mandated weight limit. When you train, you will punch your sparring partner in the stomach and head, but not below the belt. And you will also avoid throwing elbows and forearms, as these strikes will not be permitted in the ring. Finally, because your opponent is subject to these rules as well, you will not spend any of your valuable time training to defend against elbows or forearms, or against punches below the belt.

Imagine, then, that after many months of rigorous training and hard work, you go to the prefight weigh-in and drug test. You pass the drug test, and you weigh in, as expected, just under the weight limit for your class. Your opponent, however, failed the drug test by testing positive for illegal, muscle-building steroids, and also weighed in ten pounds over the weight limit. But despite all of this, the boxing regulators don't seem to care. They ignore your objections and do nothing about your opponent's gross violation of the rules. To your surprise, both his illegal-steroid and weigh-in issues are amazingly glossed over. The show must go on, they tell you.

You decide to go on with the fight, albeit under protest. And when you finally to step into the ring for the actual fight, you're in for even greater surprises. Your opponent staggers you with a barrage of elbows and forearms in the clinch, and shamelessly delivers multiple low blows right in the middle of the ring. You and your corner object, but again to no avail—much like the prefight regulators, the referee doesn't seem the least bit interested in enforcing the rules of the game. And because you trained according to the rules that prohibited elbows, forearms, and low blows, you have no idea how to defend against this attack. You're soon physically and mentally beaten. After two rounds of this illegal beat-down you are unable to answer the bell for round 3. Fight over. You lose. Your opponent is declared the champion.

To say that this would be unacceptable is a dramatic understatement. First, and most importantly, declaring your opponent the winner and champion would be incredibly unfair to you, the participant. You worked hard and followed the rules of the game, and you're entitled to a fair fight. Even if your opponent was the overwhelming prefight favorite, or even the sentimental fan favorite, no one would deny you the right to equal treatment and equal application of the rules. In fact, boxing fans and everyone else who learned of the outcome would recognize a fundamental unfairness in the way you were treated. The boxing community would be outraged on your behalf.

Second, not only would declaring your opponent the winner be incredibly unfair and unjust to you personally, but it would also be horrible for the sport of boxing. The sport of boxing, like every other sport, greatly benefits when it is perceived as fair and evenhanded. To the extent that it, or any sport, gets a reputation as being underhanded or fixed, it suffers greatly. If the rules were unevenly or selectively applied, as they were in your hypothetical championship fight, then no boxing fan could have any faith in the outcome of the fights. No one would have any reason to believe that a boxing match would produce the best fighter and true champion. The sport of boxing would soon become professional wrestling: enjoyed by some but respected by none.

So instead of letting your opponent get away with breaking nearly every imaginable rule of the game, how would the boxing referee or regulators really handle your opponent's numerous violations? The elbows, forearms, and low blows would first draw an immediate warning. Upon a second infraction, points would be deducted from your opponent's scorecard. If your opponent repeated this a third time—thereby proving either unwilling or unable to play by the rules—he would be disqualified, and you would be crowned champion. And actually, it probably wouldn't have even reached that point. Your opponent's positive prefight steroid test and failed weigh-in would have disqualified him before the fight could even begin. You might even have been awarded the champion's belt, albeit by forfeiture instead of by victory in the ring.

Rules, of course, are even more important in criminal jury trials than they are in championship fights. In fact, in keeping with our boxing analogy, the Supreme Court has even held that while the prosecutor "may strike hard blows, he is not at liberty to strike foul ones."[19] And when a prosecutor does strike foul blows—for example, by hiding evidence that he or she has a duty to turn over, striking jurors from the jury pool because of their race, intimidating or influencing witnesses, asking improper questions of witnesses, or playing on jurors' racial or other biases—the accused citizen will likely be convicted because of the prosecutor's illegal tactics.[20] After all, when people cheat they do so to gain some sort of an advantage; if cheating didn't pay, there would be no incentive to do it.

Being convicted after a tainted trial, of course, would be unfair to the individual who was entitled to a fair trial in accordance with the rules. And unlike in a boxing match, the criminal defendant who was cheated and wrongfully convicted would not only lose money, but also freedom and, in some cases and in some of our states, his or her life. But there is another loser as well. Just as the entire sport of boxing suffers when its rules are not enforced, so too does the criminal justice system when *its* rules are not enforced. When defendants are convicted because a prosecutor used illegal tactics, the financial cost of the numerous postconviction motions and appeals is not only quantifiable, but enormous. The costs of transcripts, appellate counsel for both the defendant and the state, and the use of court time and resources are borne by the taxpayer. Second, if the defendant wins a new trial because of the prosecutor's tactics, then the entire trial process has to be repeated again, which includes the cost of the prosecutor, witness fees, court time, counsel for the defendant, and other expenses.

However, as we'll see below, getting a new trial is a rare event. In fact, when defendants are convicted because of prosecutor misconduct, the convictions usually get swept under the rug by the appellate courts. When that happens, the societal costs are less easily quantified, but are even greater.[21] When prosecutors cheat, and when that cheating leads to convictions, something very harmful happens: we begin to lose confidence in our justice system—a system that prides itself not only on fair outcomes, but also the equally important *appearance* of fairness.

By analogy, after your title fight that we discussed earlier, no one would have any faith that the system produced the true boxing champion. Sure, your opponent might have been better than you, and maybe (or even probably) would have won the championship belt even without his repeated acts of cheating. But no one would be satisfied by simply giving the cheater the benefit of that doubt. He simply didn't prove it in the ring. He didn't earn it. Likewise, when prosecutors cheat and get away with it, do we really know that the prosecutor won the conviction because the defendant was truly guilty? Or did he win the conviction because he cheated, and his cheating was effective? Just as in our boxing example, we don't know if the outcome was the right one, and when we don't have faith in the outcome we begin to lose confidence in the process.

■ ■ ■

Because most criminal trials are more important than most boxing matches, shouldn't prosecutors who cheat at trial be dealt with in a fashion at least as harsh as boxers who cheat in the ring? If the prosecutor cheats, shouldn't he first be warned? And if he continues to cheat—proving that he is either unable or unwilling to play by the rules—shouldn't the defendant win an acquittal? Is that really too high a burden too put on the educated, trained, and licensed prosecutor who wields such tremendous power over us citizens? In addition to being a fair and simple approach, wouldn't this also encourage other prosecutors to play by the rules, and discourage them from cheating? Wouldn't this also save a lot of money, time, and resources in appeals and possible retrials by simply doing things right the first time?

Answers: Yes, yes, yes, no, yes, and yes. But unfortunately, the reality of the situation is quite different. In reality, the legal system deals with prosecutor misconduct using a two-step system that perversely encourages and rewards prosecutor misconduct, rather than deterring it. As you might expect, any system that perpetuates the misconduct, rather than deterring it, comes with enormous costs—some measurable and some immeasurable.

Here's how the two-step system works, in the context of a jury trial: First, when the prosecutor commits some form of misconduct—for example, by urging the jury to convict the defendant for reasons based on race or religion, rather than on the evidence—defense counsel must immediately object, and then the judge must rule on the objection. If the judge agrees with the defense lawyer that the prosecutor broke the rules, the judge will sustain the objection, which should temporarily stop the prosecutor's behavior. Conversely, if the judge disagrees with the defense lawyer, the judge will overrule the objection and let the prosecutor continue on his or her course.

Although we're only at the first step of the two-step system, it is already fundamentally flawed. In this system, the judge—who is playing the role akin to a referee in the boxing match—does nothing to maintain a fair trial. The judge merely sits back and waits for the defense lawyer to object. This is potentially dangerous to a defendant because repeated objections make defense counsel look like an obstructionist, when in fact the defense lawyer is merely trying to enforce the rules of the game. Conversely, if the defense lawyer stops objecting and the defendant is convicted at trial, the issue of prosecutor misconduct could be deemed forfeited—or, as judges say, waived—on appeal, and the defense lawyer will be blamed for not doing his or her job. Therefore, the defense lawyer must walk a fine line between, on the one hand, not alienating the jury by appearing to be an obstructionist and, on the other hand, enforcing the rules and protecting the client. (See chapter 14 for more on the ineffective assistance of counsel.) In any case, and despite the "call your own foul" approach to criminal trials, this is actually the less problematic of the two steps.

In step two of the system, if the judge has sustained the defense lawyer's objection, defense counsel must ask the judge to do something about the misconduct; that is, counsel must request a remedy to compensate for the damage caused by the prosecutor's misdeeds. Typically, the first time the prosecutor cheats, a defense lawyer won't ask for a remedy at all; just stopping the misconduct, at least temporarily, is often perceived as a victory. The second time the prosecutor cheats, the defense lawyer may ask the judge to give a special instruction to the jury to correct the misconduct, which is the functional equivalent of a warning for a low blow in boxing. If the judge grants this request, he or she may instruct the jury, for example, that despite what the prosecutor just argued, the jury must decide the case based only on the evidence, and not on issues of race or religion. This is a risky request by defense counsel, because the special instruction may do more harm than good in some circumstances. That is, it may actually draw more attention to the prosecutor's improper remarks and reinforce the prosecutor's argument, thereby exacerbating rather than correcting the problem.

In any case, if the misconduct continues, defense counsel may eventually ask for a different remedy. When the prosecutor cheats a third or fourth time, or when a single rule violation is very serious, defense counsel may ask the judge to declare a mistrial, which means that the jury is dismissed and the trial ends without a verdict. However, this is not the equivalent of a disqual- ification in boxing. When a mistrial is granted, the result, in nearly every case, is that the trial will start from scratch with a new jury. The defendant does not win by default; instead, the prosecutor is rewarded for the miscon- duct with a do-over.[22]

As unpleasant as the prospect of a new trial might sound for the defen- dant, it is often the only meaningful remedy available. After all, when the prosecutor breaks the rules he or she does so, much like the boxer who throws an elbow or forearm in the clinch, because it hurts the opponent. And once a jury has heard the misconduct—an improper, race- or religion-based argument, for example—it is impossible to un-ring the bell. Further, lesser remedies, such as the special instruction to the jury, may be ineffective at best, or even counterproductive at worst. Often, therefore, the only way to obtain a fair trial is to ask the judge to declare a mistrial and start anew.

But how does the judge decide whether to grant the defense lawyer's request and declare a mistrial? The legal test is quite bizarre, actually. The judge steps into the shoes of the jury, weighs the evidence that has been presented to that point, and decides whether the defendant would likely be convicted even had the prosecutor not committed the misconduct.[23] This test is absurd for several reasons. First, it takes away the jury's role of weighing the evidence and deciding guilt or innocence, and hands it to the trial judge. This, of course, violates the constitutional guarantee to a trial by jury. Sec- ond, the result of this test is that if the judge believes the state's evidence is strong, then he or she will find that the prosecutor's cheating wouldn't affect the verdict, and therefore the case will move forward and no mistrial will be granted.

Imagine this rule in the context of our analogous title fight in boxing. This rule is the equivalent of a referee awarding victory to your opponent after he knocks you out with an illegal elbow strike because, after all, your opponent was probably winning at the time he decided to cheat. Therefore, if he hadn't thrown the elbow, he probably would have won the fight anyway. This, of course, would never happen in boxing. But in criminal trials, it happens every day. And when prosecutors cheat and defendants are convicted, the appellate courts usually brand the constitutional violations as harmless error. That is, even though the prosecutor cheated and violated the defendant's rights, the error was harmless because the final outcome, according to the appellate court, would probably have been the same anyway. [24]

Third, and even more troubling, this test for whether to grant a mistrial actually promotes, rather than deters, prosecutor misconduct. [25] That is, if the prosecutor has a strong case to begin with and is thinking about cheating during trial, he knows that if the defendant objects and moves for a mistrial, the motion will be denied. Why? Because his evidence is already strong. As a result, the prosecutor knows that cheating during trial will just strengthen his case even further. Conversely, if the prosecutor realizes part way through trial that he is not doing well and his evidence is weak, he also has an incentive to cheat. Why? Because the worst that can happen is that the defendant will object, move for a mistrial, and get one. In that scenario, the prosecutor will get to start over and put on a better case the second time around. And if the judge denies the defendant's motion for a mistrial, then the prosecutor just strengthened what was a weak case by cheating. So regardless of whether the prosecutor has a strong case or a weak case, he is always better off if he cheats. Rules are for suckers.

The fourth and final problem with the test for whether to grant a mistrial is this: Judges get paid very large, but fixed, salaries. That is, they are not paid by the hour. How many judges do you think will want to grant a mistrial and start the case all over from square one for a defendant already convicted in the judge's own mind? Some judges will—one judge even granted a mistrial in a *four-month-long* case due to extreme prosecutorial misconduct [26] —but most judges will not. Instead, there is an incredible, built-in incentive to simply deny the request for a mistrial and do nothing—or simply issue another so-called curative instruction to the jury, which will, again, draw even more attention to the prosecutor's improper (but persuasive) misconduct.

So, in short, no matter how egregious the prosecutor's violation, it is the highly unusual case that a mistrial is granted. And, as you can now see, this test for whether to grant a mistrial does nothing to enforce the rules of a criminal trial; instead, it provides a perverse incentive for the prosecutor to cheat, and a perverse incentive for the judge to hear and see no evil. [27]

To make matters worse, even though the burden (and the risk) of objecting to the misconduct already falls on the defense lawyer, appellate courts have found creative ways to make things even more antidefendant. Appellate courts will go to extraordinary lengths to blame defense lawyers for not reacting properly to prosecutor misconduct, rather than placing the blame where it belongs: on the offending prosecutors or the lax judges. This tactic allows the appellate court to uphold, rather than reverse, the convictions, and also allows it to avoid the underlying problem altogether by sweeping it under the proverbial rug.

To demonstrate this blame-shifting tactic, assume you are convicted after a trial that was absolutely riddled with prosecutor misconduct. Your trial lawyer objected and was overruled every time by the trial judge. So you hire an appellate lawyer to appeal your conviction. After all, it wasn't a fair fight, and with all the cheating that went on you think the appellate court will have no confidence in the outcome. You soon find out, however, that the appellate court has only one goal: to preserve, rather than overturn, your conviction. And once your appellate lawyer points the finger at the prosecutor and the trial judge, the appellate court will hypercritically comb the trial transcript and look for a way to divert blame away from these two individuals by redirecting it toward your trial lawyer. If the appellate court can do that, then it can hold that you and your lawyers have waived the issues that you now raise on appeal, and you will lose again.

In doing this, the appellate court has many weapons in its arsenal. It may criticize the precise words your trial lawyer used when objecting (she didn't object with enough specificity), the precise timing of the objections (even though the misconduct was a surprise, she didn't object quickly enough), and the manner of the objections (she didn't object frequently enough or with enough vigor). The most intellectually dishonest attempt to shift blame away from the prosecutor and the judge, and toward the trial lawyer, is illustrated in the following hypothetical oral argument, which captures the precise issues from an appellate decision.[28]

Appellate Attorney: Your Honors, my client appeals his conviction due to several instances of prosecutor misconduct that occurred during trial, which are outlined in our appellate brief. The misconduct occurred in most phases of the trial, including jury selection, opening statement, examination of witnesses, and closing argument.

Appellate Court: Counsel, the trial lawyer never asked for the proper remedy: a mistrial. Therefore, he waived the issue. As you know, it is not procedurally proper to come to us on appeal and ask for a new trial when the trial lawyer never preserved the issue by asking for a mistrial.

Appellate Attorney: Your Honors, the trial lawyer never asked for mistrial because the trial judge *overruled* all of his objections. In order for the trial lawyer to ask for a remedy—whether a mistrial or some other remedy—the trial judge would first have to *sustain* an objection. Without a sustained objection, there is no basis to ask for a remedy, nor could the trial judge give a remedy because he'd just overruled the objection. In fact, had the trial lawyer requested a mistrial following an *overruled* objection, he would have been reprimanded by the trial judge in front of the jury, further hurting his client's case.

Appellate Court: Well, no. The trial lawyer could have waited until the jury was deliberating, and *then* asked for the mistrial at some point before they returned their verdict of guilt.

Appellate Attorney: Your Honors, with all due respect, that's nonsensical. First, I just told you that the judge can't give a remedy after overruling an objection. Waiting to ask for a remedy until the jury is out of the room doesn't change that. Second, if the trial lawyer had waited that long, the request would have been untimely and therefore waived anyway. The blame in this case falls on the prosecutor and the trial judge, not the trial lawyer.

Appellate Court: Thank you, Counsel. Your request for a new trial is denied. We need not address the issue of whether the prosecutor's misconduct was prejudicial as this was waived by trial counsel's failure to request a mistrial.

Appellate Attorney: Your Honors, then please analyze this issue on the basis of ineffective assistance of trial counsel for failing to request a mistrial. It's still the same issue, just with a different label.

Appellate Court: Counsel, that issue of ineffective assistance of trial counsel was not raised in your brief, and therefore *you* waived it. We will not entertain issues for the first time at oral argument. Your appeal is denied, and if your client wants he can appeal to a different court and argue ineffective assistance of *appellate* counsel for not raising the ineffective assistance of *trial* counsel. Good day.

This exchange nicely illustrates how an appellate court can parse words, hide the ball, and shift blame in order to preserve, rather than overturn, a conviction. And if all else fails, and the appellate court has to blame the prosecutor, the trial judge, or both, it can still uphold the conviction by calling it a harmless error—that is, the defendant would have been found guilty anyway, so there is no need to grant a new trial. Fairness and the appearance of fairness be damned.

■ ■ ■

By now, you might be thinking that if you're ever charged with a crime, you might just skip the trial and strike a plea bargain with the prosecutor. But land mines are lurking there as well, as we'll see in the next chapter.

NOTES

1. In addition to the rules that govern both prosecutors and defense lawyers, the prosecutor also has a special duty to "do justice" and make sure that no innocent person is prosecuted. However, because this special duty is so vague, and also directly conflicts with the prosecutor's duty to advocate for the state, it is not addressed in this book. Additionally, nearly all examples of prosecutor misconduct are cases of prosecutors violating well-known rules, not vague, pie-in-the-sky legal standards requiring that they "do justice." For a fuller discussion of this issue, including citation to relevant legal authorities, see Michael D. Cicchini, "Prosecutorial Misconduct at Trial: A New Perspective Rooted in Confrontation Clause Jurisprudence," 37 *Seton Hall Law Review* 335 (2007), available at www.CicchiniLaw.com (accessed November 19, 2011).
    2. *Brady v. Maryland*, 373 U.S. 83 (1963).
    3. *Batson v. Kentucky*, 476 U.S. 79 (1986).
    4. See *Howard v. Gramley*, 225 F.3d 784 (7th Cir. 2000).
    5. See *Kitchen v. U.S.*, 227 F.3d 1014 (7th Cir. 2000), and *U.S. v. Gardner*, 238 F.3d 878 (7th Cir. 2001).
    6. *U.S. v. Boyd*, 55 F.3d 239 (7th Cir. 1995).
    7. Ibid.
    8. See *U.S. v. Brisk*, 171 F.3d 514 (7th Cir. 1999).
    9. See *U.S. v. Cheska*, 202 F.3d 947 (7th Cir. 2000).
    10. See *Aliwoli v. Carter*, 225 F.3d 826 (7th Cir. 2000).
    11. See *Griffin v. California*, 380 U.S. 609 (1965). There are situations where a prosecutor might be permitted to argue to a jury that a defendant is guilty because he or she exercised a constitutional right, for example, his right to remain silent before trial. Usually, if the defendant is read the *Miranda* warnings and chooses to remain silent, that fact would not be admissible at trial. There are, however, exceptions. For example, if a defendant testifies that he never had the opportunity to tell his side of the story to the police, then his post-*Miranda* silence might be used to impeach him. And, interestingly, a defendant's pre-*Miranda* silence—that is, his choice to remain silent *before* the police formally read him his rights—is more likely to be admissible at trial. See *Jenkins v. Anderson*, 447 U.S. 231 (1980).
    12. Lara Setrakian and Chris Francescani, "Former Duke Prosecutor Nifong Disbarred," June 16, 2007, *ABC News*, at abcnews.go.com/TheLaw/story?id=3285862&page=1#.TsgiPcPNltM (accessed November 19, 2011).
    13. *State v. Copening*, 303 N.W.2d 821 (Wis. 1981).
    14. Ibid.
    15. *State v. Servantez*, 347 N.W.2d 352 (1984).
    16. *In the Matter of Disciplinary Proceedings Against Robert D. Zapf*, 375 N.W.2d 654 (Wis. 1985).
    17. Zapf for District Attorney, at zapfforda.com/ (accessed November 26, 2011).
    18. Interestingly, while intentionally hiding evidence of innocence might, in extreme cases, get a prosecutor in trouble with a lawyer regulatory board, merely forgetting to disclose it probably never will. However, each scenario has the same devastating impact on the defendant who had his or her rights violated.
    19. *Berger v. United States*, 295 U.S. 78, 88 (1935).

20. See Janet C. Hoeffel, "Prosecutorial Discretion at the Core: The Good Prosecutor Meets Brady," 109 *Penn State Law Review* 1133 (2005).

21. For a discussion of the financial and nonfinancial costs of prosecutor misconduct, including citations to numerous other articles, see Cicchini, "Prosecutorial Misconduct at Trial."

22. The reason that a mistrial results in retrial instead of automatic acquittal is that the Supreme Court has set up an absurd and impossible hurdle for the defendant. That is, in order for the defendant to win a postmistrial acquittal, rather than a retrial, he or she must show that the prosecutor's misconduct was designed not merely to win the case, but rather "to goad [the defendant] into requesting a mistrial" (*Oregon v. Kennedy*, 456 U.S. 667, 1982). Of course, "It is almost inconceivable that a defendant could prove that the prosecutor's deliberate misconduct was motivated by an intent to provoke a mistrial instead of an intent simply to prejudice the defendant" (Ibid.; Stevens, J., concurring).

23. See Bennett L. Gershman, "The New Prosecutors," 53 *University of Pittsburgh Law Review* 393 (1992).

24. See *State v. Servantez*, 347 N.W.2d 352 (Wis. 1984). In this homicide trial, the prosecutor withheld evidence that he was required, by law, to disclose to the defense. The appellate court reversed the conviction, but then a higher appellate court—the Wisconsin Supreme Court—reversed the lower appellate court and reinstated the conviction because, it believed, the error was harmless.

25. See Gershman, "The New Prosecutors."

26. *U.S. v. Boyd*, 55 F.3d 239 (7th Cir. 1995).

27. See Kenneth Rosenthal, "Prosecutorial Misconduct, Convictions, and Double Jeopardy: Case Studies in an Emerging Jurisprudence," 71 *Temple Law Review* 887 (1998).

28. This hypothetical dialogue is based on *State v. Smith*, No. 2005AP1617-CR (Wis. Ct. App. May 17, 2006). For a deeper discussion of the case and the issues, see Cicchini, "Prosecutorial Misconduct at Trial."

Chapter Twelve

Plea Bargaining

A Deal Is (Not) a Deal

Our popular culture would lead us to believe that criminal law takes place primarily in the courtroom. The jury trial, after all, is iconic in American culture and has long been the centerpiece of many American television shows, movies, books, and even news programs. Despite this popular image, however, the opposite is actually true. In reality, nearly all criminal cases—in some jurisdictions 95 percent of criminal cases—are resolved not by jury trial, but rather by plea bargaining.[1] It is rare, indeed, for a criminal case to actually make it through the entire criminal process and all the way to a jury trial. Instead, most are resolved over the phone, in the courthouse hallways, or on the proverbial courthouse steps—often in as little as a minute or two.

Because plea bargaining is the method by which the prosecutor obtains the vast majority of convictions, it makes sense that the Constitution would protect defendants during the plea-bargaining process. And although no defendant has the right to a plea bargain, the law says that if the prosecutor chooses to engage in plea bargaining, defendants have the right to expect the prosecutor to play fair. In other words, when the prosecutor makes a deal with a defendant, he should be required to live up to his end of the bargain.

This right to fair play is usually viewed as originating in the Fifth Amendment, and sometimes in the Sixth Amendment, of our Constitution.[2] Other times, the right to fair play is viewed as originating in simple contract law—the same body of law that governs our everyday agreements that we make outside of the criminal justice system.[3] In other words, a deal is a deal, and when we make a promise to do something we should actually do it, except under very unusual or unexpected circumstances that are out of our control. Whatever the origins of the right to fair play, however, prosecutors often fail to live up to the promises they make in the course of plea bargaining with defendants. And as you may have guessed, the law governing a prosecutor's obligations under a plea bargain is a soft law, so judges often allow prosecutors free rein to renege on their promises and agreements.

■ ■ ■

What exactly is a plea bargain? A plea bargain—the means by which the vast majority of criminal cases are resolved—is, in its simplest terms, an agreement between the prosecutor and the defendant to settle a criminal case short of a jury trial. In a plea bargain, each party promises to do something for the other.[4] While concessions by the defendant sometimes include providing valuable information or testimony for the prosecutor to use in other cases, most of the time the defendant merely agrees to plead guilty to some of the charges in his or her own criminal complaint. Concessions by the prosecutor, in turn, include some form of leniency, such as dismissal of some or even most of the charges in the criminal complaint, or a specific sentence recommendation that is favorable to the defendant.

Consider a common but simple example: Recall the unlucky woman from chapter 3, who got into an argument with her husband and son, and then grabbed her son by the arm after he swore at her and as he was leaving the room. Based on that single incident, she was charged with four crimes: (1) misdemeanor disorderly conduct; (2) felony child abuse; (3) felony false imprisonment; and (4) felony intimidation of a witness. In a case like that, assuming that the woman had no prior criminal record, the prosecutor might offer to dismiss counts 1, 2, and 4, if the woman agreed to plead guilty to count 2, the felony child abuse. Further, the prosecutor might agree to recommend to the judge, at the time of sentencing, that the woman receive probation supervision, rather than a prison or jail sentence.

If the woman accepts this plea offer, the prosecutor gets a guaranteed felony conviction for child abuse and, in return, the woman drastically reduces her potential exposure to prison time by getting the other three counts dismissed. On top of that, if the judge follows the prosecutor's recommendation—which judges often do—the woman will avoid incarceration altogether. Sure, she will be a convicted felon, and will still risk going to prison in the event that she fails while on probation. However, she probably (but not always) is better off under the plea deal than if she were to go to jury trial and get convicted of all four of the criminal counts—something that, even in cases that are strong for the defense, is a real possibility.

The above scenario partly explains why so many cases resolve by plea bargain, rather than jury trial. The system is set up not only to permit, but also to encourage, a legal form of extortion by the prosecutor. Remember, each of our state legislatures has created hundreds, if not a thousand or more, different crimes with which its citizens can be prosecuted. Further, prosecutors have virtually unchecked discretion to charge as many of these different crimes as they choose, even when there is only a single alleged incident and even when the entire affair lasted only a few seconds.[5]

Staying with our example of the woman from chapter 3: instead of charging her with one crime—say, misdemeanor disorderly conduct, which more accurately reflects her true crime, if she committed any crime at all—the prosecutor charged her with four distinct crimes for the same incident. This gives him the luxury of later plea bargaining and offering to dismiss three counts in exchange for a plea to one count. As explained above, that is quite an inducement for the defendant, considering that if she went to trial and lost she could potentially be facing something much worse. Further, even if the prosecutor had decided to charge only one crime instead of four, and the defendant wanted to go to trial on that sole allegation, the prosecutor could simply threaten to add the other three crimes unless she agreed to plead guilty to the sole allegation.[6] The legislature has given the prosecutor a tremendous arsenal of criminal charges from which to choose, and free rein to use that arsenal as aggressively as he sees fit in order to induce a plea.

This tremendous leverage, of course, puts the defendant in a very weak bargaining position, even if she is innocent. On the one hand, she can be idealistic and hold firm to the position that no innocent person should ever plead guilty to a crime. Few defendants, however, can afford to indulge in this type of naive thinking, especially if they already have criminal records. Such an indulgence would require a defendant to ignore that citizens in our country are often wrongfully convicted and incarcerated (and in some cases executed) as a result of our imperfect system of criminal justice.[7]

On the other hand, a defendant can be practical and consider the actual risks. For example, even though she is innocent, will the jury still convict her because the state's witnesses were better on the witness stand? (After all, a mere allegation, when repeated on the witness stand, is enough to convict a person of a crime.) Aside from the evidence, will the jury convict her because of her race or some other personal characteristic? Will the judge be fair and impartial, or will he punish her for taking the case to trial and wasting his valuable time? Has the overworked defense lawyer prepared the case enough to even put on a decent defense? What type of improper tactics might the prosecutor use, and will the judge let him get away with it? If she is convicted of one or more counts, will the judge hit her with the "jury tax" and punish her more than if she had simply accepted a plea deal?[8]

In most cases, the prosecutor holds all the cards, and the defendant has, by far, the most to lose. Further, the reality is that the prosecutor, and usually the trial judge as well, do not want the case to go to trial. Instead, they want it to resolve by plea bargain. After all, what prosecutor wouldn't want a guaranteed conviction rather than spending the time and effort in a trial where he could, potentially, lose on all counts? What judge would want to manage a multiday trial when he could instead dispense with the case after only a tenminute plea and sentencing hearing? The reality is that there is a tremendous downside for any defendant—regardless of whether she is factually guilty or innocent—who dares to throw a monkey wrench into this powerful government machinery.

So we know that most cases resolve by plea bargain, and we know that prosecutors and judges prefer plea bargains. Further, prosecutors reap tremendous benefits from the plea-bargaining system. Obviously, without plea bargaining a prosecutor would have to be much choosier about the types of behavior and the number of people prosecuted; that is, if a prosecutor had to take every case to trial, he or she would only be able to prosecute serious and violent crimes. No longer would prosecutors have the luxury of prosecuting spousal arguments, bounced checks, child spankings, bar scuffles, disorderly conduct, marijuana possession, operating vehicles with suspended licenses, and the myriad of other crimes where no one is hurt and there is truly no direct, or even indirect, victim of any kind.

Given the tremendous benefits that flow to prosecutors from the plea-bargaining system, it would be reasonable to think that prosecutors would be vigilant about honoring the promises they make to defendants in the course of plea bargaining, for fear that if they didn't, they might kill the goose that lays the golden eggs.[9] And even aside from the benefits of plea bargaining, it would be reasonable to think that prosecutors would honor their word out of principle alone. After all, a deal is a deal, right?

While these are all reasonable positions to hold, the reality is that sometimes prosecutors make deals and then want to renege. Sometimes a prosecutor will strike a deal under the mistaken belief that the law permits a harsher sentence than it actually does, and then later realize the mistake.[10] Other times a prosecutor may appear in court on a fellow prosecutor's case and decide that he, personally, wouldn't have struck that particular deal had he been assigned to the case from the get-go.[11] Yet other times a prosecutor may get what he bargained for from the defendant, and then decide that he just doesn't want to live up to his end of the bargain.[12]

In perhaps the best case of sour grapes, one prosecutor induced a child defendant to pay for and take a lie detector test to determine whether he committed the alleged crime. The prosecutor proposed that if the child failed the test, the child would plead to the charge; but if he passed the test, the prosecutor would dismiss the case. The child defendant accepted; and, after he paid for the test, waived his constitutional right to remain silent, and *passed* the test, the prosecutor reneged and refused to dismiss the charge. On what basis did he renege? In a very telling concession, he argued that the Constitution did not offer any protection at this stage of the criminal process; instead, "the only enforcement mechanism [was] the integrity of the parties," and presumably because the prosecutor had none, the agreement, he argued, was not enforceable. [13]

So prosecutors often want to, and do, renege on deals by using incredibly creative ways to get out of their obligations—sometimes long after the defendant has lived up to his or her end of the bargain. And, perhaps not surprisingly by this point, judges often let the prosecutors off the hook. This, in turn, violates defendants' reasonable expectations of fair play. In fact, paradoxically, because prosecutors are generally allowed free rein to abuse the plea-bargaining system, defendants actually have far fewer rights when bargaining with their freedom *inside* the criminal justice system than the rest of us do when bargaining for simple goods and services *outside* of the criminal justice system. [14]

Consider this example: Much like the woman from chapter 3, you find yourself charged with four crimes—disorderly conduct, child abuse, false imprisonment, and intimidation of a witness—all for a single family dispute that lasted about two minutes and where no one was even hurt. You hire a lawyer who indicates that, from a factual standpoint, the state may be able to prove all of these charges. But then, as you and your lawyer are preparing for your preliminary hearing—the pretrial hearing where the prosecutor has to present at least minimal evidence that you committed a felony—your lawyer receives an e-mail from the prosecutor proposing a plea bargain. The prosecutor says that if you waive the preliminary hearing, he will make a plea offer and hold it open for you until your final pretrial hearing. The offer is this: plead to misdemeanor disorderly conduct, and at sentencing the prosecutor will recommend to the judge that you receive a fine, instead of jail or probation, and he will also move to dismiss the three felony charges against you.

This sounds fantastic, you think, and your lawyer agrees. No felonies, no prison, no jail, and no probation. Sure, you'll have a criminal record, and because your spouse was a "victim" of the disorderly conduct, your crime is classified as a domestic abuse crime, and there will many collateral consequences that go along with your plea. But those are all minor concerns, in the big picture. So your attorney promptly e-mails back the prosecutor and, on your behalf, agrees to waive the preliminary hearing in order to preserve the plea bargain, and further tells the prosecutor that you accept the offer. You will enter your plea at the final pretrial hearing, which is the common practice. Then, in court the next day, you officially waive your hearing and preserve your plea offer on the record and in front of the court commissioner. The commissioner then gives you your final pretrial hearing date in front of the judge assigned to your case.

In order to complete your end of the deal, all you'll have to do is plead guilty to the disorderly conduct, as you promised. Your lawyer was a bit surprised by this plea offer. This resolution was quick, easy, and pretty darn good compared to what she's used to seeing; in other words, the prosecutor was unusually reasonable. The whole thing seems almost unnatural. In any case, if all goes according to plan, the judge will give you a fine (though as we'll see in chapter 13, your judge may not be bound to follow any specific sentence recommendation), your three felonies will be dismissed, and you'll be on your merry way after only a brief foray into our criminal justice system.

When the morning of your final pretrial hearing arrives, however, the prosecutor with whom you made your plea deal isn't in court; instead, a different prosecutor is there. When the judge calls your case, you and your attorney step up to the defense table and you each take a seat. The judge asks for the status of your case, and your attorney states that it has been resolved for a plea to disorderly conduct and a fine recommendation from the prosecutor. Your attorney also states that you're ready to enter your plea and resolve the case today—no doubt welcome news for a judge with a clogged court calendar.

The new prosecutor, however, who just looked at your file for the first time about two minutes ago, decides that he doesn't like you or the plea deal made by the first prosecutor, and he isn't going to honor it. But you don't have the courage or the money to fight the state over three felony charges, and you really want the plea offer that you've already accepted. As you start to panic, the in-court dialogue goes like this:

Prosecutor: Judge, the plea offer was never formally accepted by the defendant, and I'm withdrawing it today. As the court knows, basic contract law says that anyone who makes an offer can withdraw it at any time before it is formally accepted. Instead, this defendant can plead to one of the felonies, or take the case to trial if he's bold enough.

Defense Lawyer: Judge, the prosecutor is right, that is a general rule of contract law, but the fact is that we *did* accept it, just a minute ago, before he tried to withdraw it. And on top of that, we accepted it by a return e-mail, just minutes after the offer was made; here's a printed copy of the offer and acceptance. This is a done deal.

Prosecutor: Well, none of that matters because *I* don't want the deal. I didn't make this offer and I'm not honoring it. He's dealing with *me* now.

Defense Lawyer: Judge, that's wrong. He understands contract law and knows full well that *he* is not the plaintiff in this case, but rather *the state* is. And every prosecutor is an agent of the state and can bind the state to plea-bargain deals. That's what the first prosecutor did, and a second prosecutor can't renege just because he doesn't like the deal made by the first prosecutor.[15] You'll also notice that this prosecutor changed his reasons for trying to renege: first he said that the defendant didn't accept the offer, and now he's saying that he just doesn't like the deal.

You're really impressed with your lawyer. You didn't hire her to deal with contract issues, but she really knows her stuff, and she's making the prosecutor look silly. (It also helps that this particular prosecutor talks first and thinks, if at all, second.) You're quite confident, at this point, that the judge is going to rule in your favor and hold the state to its end of the bargain. After all, fair is fair, and a deal is a deal. But the prosecutor isn't done yet:

Prosecutor: Judge, that doesn't matter either. There is no detrimental reliance; that is, the defendant never did anything in reliance on the plea offer. Therefore, we can withdraw it at any time, and that's what I'm doing.

Defense Lawyer: Judge, detrimental reliance is not even an issue when we have a fully formed contract, as we do here. On top of that, my client *did* detrimentally rely on the plea offer by waiving the preliminary hearing. When a person gives up something to which he or she has a legal right, *that* is detrimental reliance. In fact, the first prosecutor specifically required that we give up our preliminary hearing in exchange for this offer, which we have already accepted.[16]

Prosecutor: Wait, wait, Judge! That's all out the window too. In reviewing our file, it shows that this defendant has a prior reckless-driving conviction. We would never have made that offer had the defense disclosed that information to us. We are entitled to get out of this deal due to the defendant's misrepresentation.[17]

Defense Lawyer: First, the prosecutor is referring to an ordinance violation for reckless driving, not a criminal conviction. Second, there was never a misrepresentation about anything; no one ever asked about my client's history of driving tickets, nor would anyone have a reason to. And third, the prosecutor had that information in his file *before* he made the plea offer to us. I know that because he turned it over to me, as he is required to do, before he made the offer. Judge, we've wasted enough time on this. Enough is enough. Please enforce this plea agreement so we can resolve this case and move on. We all have other things we need to be doing.

This, you think, is going unbelievably well. The prosecutor doesn't have a leg to stand on, and your lawyer has covered every base. Your confidence grows, and you now fully expect to wrap this up today for the deal that you made with the first prosecutor. But we're still not done:

Prosecutor: Judge, the bottom line is that the defendant never entered a plea. Until the plea is entered in open court, the Constitution offers no protection for a defendant. I'm withdrawing the offer before that point.[18]

Defense Lawyer: First he changed his excuses, and now he's changing from contract law to constitutional law. It is true that the Constitution offers more protection after the plea is entered, and my client has not yet entered a plea in this case even though he's been trying to do so for the last fifteen minutes. However, the Constitution still protects us from the prosecutor's bad faith, and that's exactly what we have here. He keeps making up these excuses and throwing them at the wall, hoping something will stick. That's bad faith. We can enforce this under basic contract law and under the Constitution.

Judge: All right, all right, I've heard enough. The state can withdraw an offer anytime before the plea is entered in open court. After the plea is entered, then the prosecutor has to live with it. But there is no enforceable plea bargain in our case. Because the case is not resolved, it's going to trial. Ms. Clerk, give them a trial date.

Defense Lawyer: Judge, that's not an accurate statement of the law on plea bargaining. Let me brief this issue for the court . . .

Judge: No, I've ruled. Ms. Clerk, give them a trial date. If your client decides to take the prosecutor's new offer of pleading to a felony, please notify the court and we'll change the trial date to a plea and sentencing hearing.

What the hell just happened? Now you've got to wait months, or maybe even a year or more, before you'll get your trial and the case is finally resolved. You'll also have to pay thousands of dollars in additional attorney's fees. You'll have to continue to live under your bond conditions, including the "no contact" order that prohibits you from seeing your family. This means that you'll have to maintain two residences, which will double your family expenses. You also risk losing at trial, which could result in felony convictions and maybe even prison time. On top of all of that, this hot-to-trot prosecutor is treating you like the criminal of the century and, for some reason, is looking to make life miserable for you over a two-minute argument with your wife and son.

Then you start to wonder, what if you had entered your plea just seconds before this prosecutor had a chance to study his file and renege on the deal? The judge said, "After the plea is entered, then the prosecutor has to live with it." Well, it might not have mattered, despite the judge's rhetoric. If you had actually entered your plea, and the prosecutor still wanted to get out of the deal, the judge could have just changed the legal standard—and moved the target on you—in order to benefit the prosecutor.

For example, instead of focusing on when a "plea is entered in open court" as the triggering event, the judge could focus on something different. He could decide, for example, that it's okay for the prosecutor to renege, even after you've entered your plea. Why? Because the statements and other information you provided during the plea hearing—including your admission of guilt in open court—could not be used by the prosecutor in your upcoming trial. Therefore, the prosecutor did not unfairly benefit at your expense, and should be allowed to renege on the plea deal.[19] In reality, of course, this would be totally irrelevant to whether you had a binding agreement. However, as the facts change, so does the legal standard. By constantly moving the target, prosecutors and judges are more easily able to bypass your constitutional and contractual rights that would otherwise permit you to enforce your plea bargain.

You now get an idea of how plea bargaining works. If you're a defendant, a prosecutor has enough weaponry in the arsenal, and enough leverage when using it, to force you into a plea that you really don't want but, on the other hand, that you can't afford to turn down. That's why 95 percent of all criminal cases are resolved by plea bargains. Conversely, if you get a plea offer that seems too good to be true, it probably is. The prosecutor can simply renege on the deal for any or no reason if he happens to change his mind. Further, although a plea bargain is nothing more than a contract between two parties—here, the defendant and the state—judges will often suspend the law of contracts, and ignore the Constitution, in order to give the prosecutor a way out of plea-bargain obligations.

■ ■ ■

Despite the bad outcome in your hypothetical attempt at enforcing your plea bargain, we saw in this chapter that your defense lawyer was really on the ball and, by any objective standard, completely out-dueled the prosecutor in the courtroom. Sometimes, however, that is not the case. Sometimes, defense lawyers don't perform quite that well. And if your lawyer performs too poorly, the Constitution might protect you, as it guarantees your right to the effective assistance of counsel. Just how much does your lawyer have to do to be considered "effective," thus satisfying your constitutional right? Surprisingly little, as chapter 14 will show. But first, let's complete the criminal process and discuss sentencing, which is the topic of chapter 13.

NOTES

1. For statistics on the number of cases that are resolved by plea bargain as opposed to jury trial, see Julian A. Cook III, "All Aboard! The Supreme Court, Guilty Pleas, and the Railroading of Criminal Defendants," 75 *University of Colorado Law Review* 863 (2004).

2. For the constitutional origins of the right to fair play and fair dealing by the prosecutor, see *Cooper v. United States*, 594 F.2d 12 (4th Cir. 1979).

3. For the contract-law origin of the right to fair play and fair dealing by the prosecutor, see *U.S. v. Fields*, 766 F.2d 1161 (7th Cir. 1985).

4. See *State v. Thompson*, 426 A.2d 14, 15 n.1 (Md. Ct. Spec. App. 1981), which defines plea bargaining as "any agreement between the prosecutor and the defendant whereby a defendant agrees to perform some act or service in exchange for more lenient treatment by the prosecutor."

5. See *State v. Rabe*, 291 N.W.2d 809 (1980).

6. See *U.S. v. Goodwin*, 457 U.S. 368 (1982), and *Bordenkircher v. Hayes*, 434 U.S. 357 (1978).

7. See The Innocence Project, at www.innocenceproject.org/ (accessed November 19, 2011).

8. See Michael D. Cicchini, "The Jury Tax," the Legal Watchdog, August 13, 2011, at thelegalwatchdog.blogspot.com/2011/08/jury-tax.html (November 19, 2011).

9. For a discussion of how reneging on plea bargains may jeopardize the benefits that prosecutors receive from the plea bargaining system, see Peter Westen and David Westin, "A Constitutional Law of Remedies for Broken Plea Bargains," 66 *California Law Review* 471 (1978).

10. See *Jackson v. Schneider*, 86 P.3d 381 (Ariz. Ct. App. 2004).

11. See *State v. Scott*, 602 N.W.2d 296 (Wis. Ct. App. 1999).

12. See *State v. Brockman*, 357 A.2d 376 (Md. 1976).

13. *In re Kenneth H.*, 95 Cal. Rptr. 2d 5 (2000).

14. See Michael D. Cicchini, "Broken Government Promises: A Contract-Based Approach to Enforcing Plea Bargains," 38 *New Mexico Law Review* 159 (2008).

15. See *State v. Scott*.

16. See *People v. Macrander*, 756 P.2d 356 (Colo. 1988); compare *State v. Beckes*, 300 N.W.2d 871 (Wis. Ct. App. 1980).

17. See *State v. Bourland*, 862 P.2d 457 (N.M. Ct. App. 1993).

18. For a discussion of the origins and limits of constitutional protections in the plea-bargaining process, see *Santobello v. New York*, 404 U.S. 257 (1971); *Mabry v. Johnson*, 467 U.S. 504 (1984); and *Cooper v. United States*, 594 F.2d 12 (4th Cir. 1979).

19. See *United States v. Ocanas*, 628 F.2d 353 (5th Cir. 1980); and *United States v. Thalman*, 457 F. Supp. 307 (E.D. Wis. 1978).

Chapter Thirteen

Sentencing

Let the Punishment Exceed the Crime

If a defendant strikes a plea agreement with the prosecutor, or if he goes to trial and is found guilty of one or more of the charges against him, he will end up a convicted criminal. And once a defendant is convicted, the trial judge gets to sentence him. It is possible for some defendants to receive a monetary penalty (a fine) as their only punishment. It is also possible, and even somewhat common, for some defendants to have their sentences withheld, and instead receive probation supervision. However, many defendants convicted of a crime will, either immediately or eventually, be sent off to a county jail or a state penitentiary. And when a defendant is sentenced to a term of incarceration, the Constitution is supposed to ensure, roughly speaking, that the punishment fits the crime.[1] In reality, however, the punishment often far exceeds the crime, when measured against any imaginable standard.

■ ■ ■

A sentence of incarceration can be for as little as one day in the county jail, or as long as life imprisonment without the possibility of parole. If a defendant is convicted of punching someone and causing pain or a bruise, commonly known as misdemeanor battery, he or she might be facing incarceration of up to nine months or a year. If convicted of grabbing someone and (even temporarily) restraining that person, commonly known as false imprisonment, he or she might be facing incarceration of up to six years. If convicted (even as a teenager) of having consensual sexual contact with a fifteen-year-old, commonly known as sexual assault of a child, he or she might be facing incarceration of up to forty years, along with a staggering host of so-called collateral consequences. (These collateral consequences might include such things as lifetime probation supervision, draconian sex-offender supervision, lifetime reporting on the sex-offender registry, or, worse yet, even lifetime civil commitment as a sex offender.)

Although there now a dizzying array of federal crimes, most crimes and their penalties are creations of our state governments. And while the names of the crimes and their accompanying penalties will vary from state to state, one thing is fairly consistent: in most states, and for most crimes, judges have a tremendous amount of discretion in doling out punishment. In other words, our state legislatures have given judges nearly unfettered freedom to lock people up for as long as they wish, provided their sentences fall within the incredibly broad legal limits. And all the judge has to do to justify a sentence is to set forth some basic nondiscriminatory reasons on the record. And even if the sentencing judge fails to do that, and the defendant appeals the sentence, the appellate court will start with a strong presumption that the judge's sentence was reasonable, and will look for any reason to uphold it. [2]

Judges in our country aren't shy about using their broad discretion and punitive powers. They love to lock people up for more things, and for longer periods of time, than judges in any other part of the world. [3] At the time that I write this, there are currently about 2.5 million people incarcerated in the United States, and no other nation comes close in either the total number of citizens or the percentage of citizens who are locked up. Some observers have described our judges' obsession with crime and punishment, especially in the context of our so-called war on drugs, as "ignorant fanaticism." [4]

Shocking examples of excessive sentences abound. We learned in chapter 10 about the bribe-taking judge who went out of his way to ensure that some defendants—those who weren't paying him bribes—would be sentenced to death. And he wasn't the only judge to succumb to the almighty dollar. In Pennsylvania, two judges were taking millions of dollars from the builder and owner of a for-profit incarceration facility. [5] Why would a private, for-profit jail want to pay these judges so much money—or any money at all, for that matter? Because the judges would return the favor by filling up the for-profit jails with the children who appeared before them in juvenile court. Even minor offenses would land the juveniles in lockup, and would put money in the judges' pockets in the scheme that became known as "kids for cash." [6] But don't worry for the kids. When one of the judges was convicted and sentenced for his life-ruining crimes, he made things all better: "My actions undermined your faith in the system and contributed to the difficulty in your lives." [7] Do you think? In the end, "the Pennsylvania Supreme Court overturned about 4,000 juvenile convictions."[8] But while that looks good on paper, it was likely too little, too late, as most of the children had already served their excessive sentences.

But aside from these extreme abuses, and even aside from our nation's ongoing use of the death penalty—a topic that would require an entire book of its own—our criminal justice system routinely (and legally) sends even nonviolent offenders to state penitentiaries for many years, decades, or even life. One of the most extreme examples is California's budget-crippling "three strikes and you're in" law, where people have been incarcerated for life terms for things as minor as petty theft.[9] But, in fairness, that particular slow-moving train wreck was actually caused by California's legislature, and not its judges. That is, California lawmakers drafted a politically popular (at the time) law, and judges often didn't have any choice but to follow it and incarcerate defendants for unreasonable periods of time.

The balance of this chapter, however, is devoted to ways in which judges, rather than legislators, use their discretion to justify imposing lengthy or even maximum periods of confinement when sentencing defendants. Three of these judicial techniques are rather run-of-the-mill, and therefore we'll briefly dispense with them here.

First, if a defendant is about to be sentenced and already has a criminal record, a judge can rely on those past convictions to justify ramping up the length of the sentence he or she is about to impose. Sometimes the state legislature has even passed a statute that specifically permits the judge to go beyond the normal maximum penalty for the current crime, as if the already incredibly broad sentencing range didn't give the judge enough room in which to operate.[10]

Second, sometimes a defendant will be convicted of multiple crimes for a single act. An excellent example of this is the "reckless" type of crime, such as reckless driving, where no one was hurt but several people were potentially put at risk of harm. In a case like this, a prosecutor can charge and convict a defendant of separate crimes for each person who was in the area during the time of the defendant's conduct. And when that happens, a judge can sentence the defendant to multiple, *consecutive* sentences for the single act that led to the multiple convictions.[11] In a case like that, the number of years of imprisonment can add up fast.

Third, when doling out punishment, judges can consider not only the crime of conviction, but also crimes that were dismissed and "read in" at sentencing. When a criminal charge is dismissed and read in, that means that the defendant cannot be sentenced for it, but the judge can consider it when determining the appropriate sentence for the actual crime of conviction. On top of that, judges can even base their sentences on crimes for which the defendant was never even charged, let alone convicted—this is called "considering the defendant's character," which is a relevant sentencing factor. But if the defendant was never convicted or even charged, how does the judge know that the defendant did anything wrong? He doesn't, of course. He just assumes the uncharged allegations to be true based on the prosecutor's unfounded assertions.

But there are even more Machiavellian ways in which judges can justify imposing incredibly lengthy sentences, or even justify incarcerating people who shouldn't be incarcerated at all. In the sections to follow we'll discuss two of these techniques, starting with the "jury tax."

■ ■ ■

The law states that a criminal defendant cannot be penalized merely for exercising a constitutional right, such as a jury trial.[12] But as defense lawyers know, penalties can sometimes be harsher if a defendant passes on a plea deal and instead proceeds to trial, and loses. This isn't always the case; in fact, because criminal statutes today cover such a broad range of innocuous behavior, it's sometimes better for a defendant to have a trial, even if he or she ends up losing. This way, the judge can see just how mitigated the "crime" actually was, and might take that into account when pronouncing sentence. But the risk of receiving a harsher penalty for going to trial and losing—also known as the jury tax—is alive and well.

A prime example of the jury tax can be seen in *State v. Strupp*, where the defendant lost at jury trial and then received a twenty-year sentence.[13] When pronouncing sentence, the trial judge relied in part on the defendant's perjurous testimony at trial—after all, the jury rejected his theory of defense and convicted him, so the defendant must have lied on the witness stand. But even the prosecutor had to jump in and correct the judge: this defendant had remained silent, and never even testified at trial. (Which makes one wonder: what was the judge doing during the trial?) The judge then slightly changed his approach and said that he was instead relying on the defendant's bogus trial defense of self-defense. This time, the defense lawyer had to jump in and correct the judge, reminding him that self-defense was his (the lawyer's) trial strategy, that is, a matter left up to the lawyer and outside the defendant's control.

The court nonetheless imposed a twenty-year sentence, and on appeal the defendant argued that this was an impermissible jury tax; in other words, the judge was punishing him merely for exercising his constitutional right to put the state to its burden of proof at trial. The appellate court, however, took a different view. Even though "the [trial judge] was twice corrected by the prosecutor and defense attorney," the appellate court bent over backward to uphold the sentence: "we read the court's remarks in total as revealing its reliance, not on any specific assertion about intent by Strupp, but instead on Strupp's general failure to take responsibility."[14]

So it all boils down to "taking responsibility." But isn't failing to take responsibility the same thing as going to trial? Imagine if the defendant had told the trial judge, after losing at trial, that he was very sorry and took full responsibility for his actions. Would the judge have been impressed? Of course not. The judge would have rejected this, and would have pointed out that if the defendant really took responsibility, he wouldn't have put everyone through a jury trial.

In fact, the only action that could possibly be construed as taking responsibility is taking a plea deal. So when the appellate court says that a trial judge can dole out a harsh sentence because the defendant failed to take responsibility, that's just another way of saying that the trial judge can punish a defendant for going to trial—because having a trial is, of course, the opposite of taking responsibility.

And this leads to an interesting subissue. Although having a trial is the very definition of not taking responsibility, the inverse fails to hold true; that is, taking a plea deal is not the definition of taking responsibility. Why? Because when defendants take plea deals, there is nearly always some concession by the state—for example, if a defendant pleads to three counts, the state will dismiss one count. And when defendants take such deals, judges typically reject defendants' claims that they are taking responsibility for their actions. Why? Because, the judges say, these defendants are not really taking responsibility, but instead are merely acting out of self-interest; that is, they are taking plea deals only to get reduced charges or other concessions from the state.

This all leads to the question, how can a defendant truly take responsibility? The answer: plead straight up to every charge in a multicount complaint (even when all charges stem from a single act of alleged wrongdoing), repent profusely, and ask for consecutive sentences of the maximum penalties that the particular state's legislature, in all its wisdom, permits.

On second thought, the jury trial is preferable, jury tax and all.

■ ■ ■

Jury tax aside, a basic sense of fairness dictates that a criminal defendant should be sentenced only for the crime of conviction. Given this, most people would be surprised to learn that, as discussed earlier, judges may also consider uncharged and unproved offenses when dispensing punishment, and increase their sentences accordingly. But this incredibly lax standard still wasn't enough for one judge, who went even further and created facts out of thin air (and contrary to the evidence) to justify sending an autistic defendant to prison. [15]

In *State v. DeVera*, the twenty-one-year-old defendant suffered from "several developmental disorders," including a form of autism "which manifests, in part, as a child-like presentation and social immaturity." [16] This defendant had an ongoing, "non-coercive" sexual relationship with his girlfriend, which led to a felony charge of statutory rape. [17] The state offered a lesser felony and a recommendation for probation, which the defendant accepted. At sentencing, however, the judge ignored the parties' joint request for probation, and instead ordered nine years' imprisonment because, as the judge repeated several times, the defendant "already had proved his unsuitability for probation by flouting conditions of probation and bail." [18]

Normally, "flouting conditions of probation and bail" would be good reasons for considering a prison sentence; however, as the defense lawyer told the judge at the hearing, this defendant had never before been convicted of a crime, let alone placed on probation. Further, because he didn't have $25,000 in cash, he was never even released on bail; instead, he was brought to court in a jumpsuit—compliments of the county jail where he had been sitting for the eight months leading up to sentencing.

Because the judge sentenced this young man to prison for violating probation and bail when, in reality, he had never been placed on either one, the appellate court reversed the sentence. And on paper, at least, everything turned out the way it was supposed to, albeit three years too late. After the appellate attorney won the reversal, she wisely filed a substitution request for a different judge at resentencing. Then, the defense attorney at resentencing persuaded the new judge to order probation. But what about the three years— that's right, *three years*—that the disabled defendant spent in prison because the first sentencing judge decided to make up facts and destroy his life as he knew it? Well, nothing. Those are three years that are lost forever. Even worse, there's no way to tell what kind of harmful effects his prison experience will have on him in the future.

Reversals of sentences are incredibly rare. In fact, in this case, when reversing the prison sentence, the appellate court stated that it would have upheld the sentence had the sentencing judge not made up facts, but instead offered different reasons—any reasons—to support the sentence. So, in that sense, this defendant is very lucky. There are hundreds of defendants who won't get their lengthy prison sentences reversed simply because their sentencing judges were crafty enough to support their draconian sentences with reasons that, although pretextual, were impossible for defendants to disprove with 100 percent certainty.

Interestingly, and proving that truth is indeed stranger than fiction, the sentencing judge who sent this young, developmentally disabled defendant to prison for having consensual sexual contact with his girlfriend was soon thereafter accused of her own crime.[19] The district attorney charged her with disorderly conduct for allegedly committing a string of violent and dangerous public acts—including screaming in public, jumping onto moving cars, and even driving her own car recklessly through a residential neighborhood—all in an attempt to track down her ex-lover. Did she get a lengthy prison sentence, much like the kind she was used to doling out for things far less violent and dangerous than her own alleged behavior? Did she get some jail time? Did she at least get probation, including mandatory counseling?

The answer to all of the above is no. For some reason, the prosecutor only charged Her Honor with a single-count misdemeanor complaint to begin with, and then he further reduced that single count to a noncriminal ordinance violation—also known as a ticket—in the course of plea bargaining.[20] She was sentenced to pay a $100 forfeiture, which is the civil equivalent of a criminal fine.[21] If only defendants who aren't judges could get such plumb deals.

■ ■ ■

So there you have it. With an arsenal of sentencing techniques like the ones discussed in this chapter, it's no wonder that our prison population dwarfs that of every other nation.

Now that we've taken aim at police, prosecutors, and judges, there's one more target to explore: defense lawyers themselves. This is the topic of the next chapter.

NOTES

1. See United States Constitution, Eighth Amendment, at www.law.cornell.edu/constitution/eighth_amendment (accessed November 26, 2011), which states that "[e]xcessive bail shall not be required, nor excessive fines imposed, nor cruel and unusual punishments inflicted."

2. See *State v. Gallion*, 2004 WI 42.

3. Adam Liptak, "Inmate Count in U.S. Dwarfs Other Nations'," *New York Times*, April 23, 2008, at www.nytimes.com/2008/04/23/us/23prison.html (accessed March 26, 2010).

4. Ibid.

5. Associated Press, "Ex-Judge Gets 17 1/2 Years in Pa. Kickbacks Case," *Tribune Chronicle*, September 24, 2011, at www.tribune-chronicle.com/page/content.detail/id/147488/Ex-judge-gets-17-1-2-years-in-Pa--kickbacks-case-.html?isap=1&nav=5029 (accessed December 3, 2011).

6. Ibid.

7. Ibid.

8. Ibid.

9. Bill Mears, "Supreme Court Upholds Long Sentences under Three-Strikes-You're-Out Law," *CNN*, March 5, 2003, at edition.cnn.com/2003/LAW/03/05/scotus.three.strikes/index.html (accessed November 26, 2011).

10. For a discussion of Wisconsin's penalty-enhancer statutes, see, for example, *State v. Upchurch*, 305 N.W.2d 57 (Wis. 1981); and *State v. Jackson*, 2004 WI 29.

11. For a discussion of consecutive sentences generally, see, for example, *State v. Thums*, 2006 WI App. 173.

12. The section on the jury tax is a reprint, with minor modifications, of Michael D. Cicchini, "The Jury Tax," the Legal Watchdog, August 13, 2011, at thelegalwatchdog.blogspot.com/2011/08/jury-tax.html (accessed November 27, 2011).

13. *State v. Strupp*, Wis. Ct. App. 2010AP1806-CR (2011).

14. Ibid.

15. The section on creative sentencing is a reprint, with minor modifications, of Michael D. Cicchini, "Judge Makes Up Facts and Sends Autistic Defendant to Prison," the Legal Watchdog, November 28, 2010, at thelegalwatchdog.blogspot.com/2010/11/judge-makes-up-facts-and-sends-autistic.html (accessed November 27, 2011).

16. State v. DeVera, Wis. Ct. App., 2010AP126-CR (2011).

17. Ibid.

18. Ibid.

19. Michael D. Cicchini, "Linda Van De Water: Poor Judge(ment)?" the Legal Watchdog, April 9, 2011, at thelegalwatchdog.blogspot.com/2011/04/linda-van-de-water-poor-judgement.html (accessed December 3, 2011).

20. Wisconsin Circuit Court Access, at wcca.wicourts.gov/caseDetails.do;jsessionid=849DE7E3062798DD4E5FF448131D588E.render6?caseNo=2011CM0007 28&countyNo=51&cacheId=3BB9B7D9AB0C621918DCEDD850720604&recordCount=4& offset=0 (accessed December 3, 2011).

21. Wisconsin Circuit Court Access, at http://wcca.wicourts.gov/courtRecordEvents.xsl;jsessionid=849DE7E3062798DD4E5FF448131D588E.render6?caseNo=2011CM000 728&countyNo=51&cacheId=3BB9B7D9AB0C621918DCEDD850720604&recordCount=4& offset=0&linkOnlyToForm=false&sortDirection=DESC (accessed December 3, 2011).

Chapter Fourteen

You Have the Right to the (Effective) Assistance of Counsel

The Constitution guarantees, at least in theory, that every person charged with a crime receives the effective assistance of counsel in defense of the allegation.[1] This is true whether the person hires a private attorney and pays a million-dollar retainer, or is indigent and qualifies for public-defender representation. Regardless, the defense attorney must have a certain minimal level of competence, and must demonstrate a certain minimal level of effort in the case, in order satisfy the constitutional right to the effective assistance of counsel.[2] But the meaning of the word effective, as you might suspect, is rather soft and malleable.

■ ■ ■

In some cases, defending a client accused of a crime can be incredibly difficult, complex, stressful, and draining. This is especially true given the adversarial nature of the criminal justice system—not only between defense counsel and the prosecutor, but, in some cases, between defense counsel and the judge, the witnesses, and even his or her own client. Additionally, the defense lawyer must make literally dozens of difficult strategic decisions throughout the course of a case. These decisions sometimes begin before a criminal complaint is even filed, and certainly continue throughout the criminal process, including pretrial motions, case investigation, plea negotiations, and especially jury trial. Each decision carries with it the possibility that a single misstep could cost the client his or her freedom and, in some cases and in some states, even his or her life.

To make matters even worse, many lawyers, despite being licensed and regulated professionals, received virtually no training in how to actually *practice* law. Unlike medical schools, law schools generally do *not* train their students to practice their profession.[3] In fact, some law professors take great pride in this fact by boldly claiming, first, that they can somehow separate the theoretical aspects of the law from its practical aspects, and, second, that their job is simply to teach the theoretical portion.[4] Some professors, therefore, are not concerned with (or might even be incapable of) imparting the practical knowledge and skills required for actual legal practice. Instead, they have their own agendas and pursue legal topics—both inside and outside of the classroom—that interest them personally, without regard to the interests of their students or anyone else in the legal community.[5]

It is true that nearly all law schools today have some clinical-practice opportunities or at least offer some practice-based courses, such as legal drafting, trial advocacy, and appellate advocacy. However, these types of courses and programs are usually *not* integrated into the schools' overall educational plan; rather, they are usually treated as separate and distinct components, often taught by part-time faculty, and they are disjointed and too narrowly focused to provide the comprehensive education necessary to teach students how to practice law.

On top of that, these practice-based courses are rarely, if ever, required. Instead, whether to take them is left entirely up to the students themselves. This means that students can, and often do, go through three years of law school without any hint of practical training or experience. Then these newly minted law-school graduates will take a two-day, purely academic test—the bar exam—that is no different in substance or style from a law-school exam. Based solely on that exam, they are instantly licensed to practice law and render legal services of all kinds, including criminal-defense representation. Sometimes there is not even a requirement to have taken a criminal procedure class before actually practicing criminal law, where real lives will hang in the balance. (Thankfully, medical schools are operated with a much more practice-driven approach to education.)

Many believe that the existing law-school format is, in and of itself, ineffective and desperately in need of revamping.[6] Further, the justification for law schools teaching only legal theory—or, as some call it, teaching students to "think like a lawyer"—is increasingly coming under attack. The fact is, as earlier chapters in this book have demonstrated, many lawyers have emerged from law school "thinking" as weakly, and in as unstructured a fashion, as when they first entered law school—and many of these lawyers become prosecutors, and then grow up to be judges.

But despite the lack of training, and the incredibly difficult nature of the defense lawyer's job, the right to the effective assistance of counsel, much like the other rights discussed in this book, is supposed to be a fundamental constitutional guarantee. Also, much like the other rights discussed in this book, the right to the effective assistance of counsel is soft and flexible, and is often destroyed by prosecutors and judges. How could a prosecutor or judge be responsible for a defendant not receiving the effective assistance of his or her own lawyer? The next section will illustrate how this most commonly occurs.

■ ■ ■

Suppose, once again, that you are charged with a crime. You get a trial attorney—whether privately retained or state appointed—and things go badly for you. Maybe you entered into a plea deal and got a harsher sentence than you anticipated. Maybe you went to trial and were convicted. Whatever happened, it was bad, or at least worse than you expected. So you then hire an appellate attorney, or, if you were sent to jail or prison and you've run out of money, maybe the public defender's office will appoint one for you at the state's expense.

This appellate attorney should review what happened in your case—which includes inspecting the pleadings, any pretrial motions, the court record, and the transcript of the proceedings—and decide if the judge or prosecutor did anything to violate your rights. If so, you may have reason to appeal. This, in turn, might get you a new sentencing hearing, a new trial, or even the dismissal of your charges. But on top of that, the appellate attorney will also look to see if your trial lawyer did, or failed to do, something in your case that rendered his or her performance below the standard of effective assistance that is guaranteed by the Constitution. If so, you may be entitled to the same remedy—for example, a new trial—on this basis as well. This is not, however, a lawsuit against your trial lawyer. Rather, this is merely your request—to the trial judge, the appellate court, or both—for some remedy in your criminal case because your trial lawyer failed to live up to the minimum standards prescribed by the Constitution.

The test for whether you received ineffective assistance of counsel is this: first, your trial lawyer must have performed deficiently in some way; and second, that deficiency must have caused you some type of harm.[7] Your argument—first to the trial judge and then, if the trial judge disagrees with you, to the appellate court—is essentially that your trial lawyer screwed up, and because of that screwup, you were harmed. Typically, this harm comes in the form of a guilty verdict and a conviction, instead of an acquittal, after a jury trial.

There will first be a court hearing on this issue in front of the trial judge. At that hearing, your new appellate lawyer will probably subpoena your old trial lawyer to the witness stand, ask him questions, and try to prove that he was ineffective in the things he did or didn't do, or in the decisions that he made throughout your case. For example, maybe he didn't do any independent investigation about the facts of the case. Maybe he didn't even read the police reports or witness statements before trial. Maybe he forgot to subpoena a witness who could have helped your case. Maybe he didn't cross-examine a witness properly by failing to point out his inconsistent stories for the jury. Or maybe he fell asleep on the job—either figuratively or literally, which happens more often than you would think[8]—and he allowed the prosecutor to get away with misconduct to which he should have objected.

At this court hearing, something very strange will happen: there will be a bizarre and almost unholy alliance among your trial lawyer, the judge, and the prosecutor. First, your old defense lawyer will usually want to defend himself and his decisions when he testifies, and he'll give reasons for why he did or didn't do the thing that you're now bringing up. In some ways this is natural and understandable; no one wants to be labeled as ineffective in his job. Second, the prosecutor will want to build up your trial lawyer's performance and argue that he was not only effective by constitutional standards, he was, in fact, *brilliant*. Why? Because if the judge agrees with the prosecutor and rules that your trial lawyer was effective, rather than ineffective, then you lose your hearing and your conviction stands. Third and finally, there is the trial judge. What do you think he'll want to do? Do you think he'll want to rule that your trial lawyer was ineffective at trial, give you a new trial, and then go through the whole multiday or multiweek affair for a second time? That is doubtful, to say the least.

But there's more bad news for you. First, with regard to proving that your trial lawyer screwed up, there is a strong legal presumption that your trial lawyer's performance was legally sufficient, or effective. You might remember the word presumption from chapter 5. Essentially, in this situation, it means that the courts will "give great deference to counsel's performance, and, therefore, a defendant must overcome a strong presumption that counsel acted reasonably within the professional norms."[9] This is a high hurdle for a defendant to clear.

Second, even assuming the court agrees that you trial lawyer screwed up, you and your appellate lawyer also have to convince the court that it was the screwup—and not something else, such as your guilt—that led to your conviction at trial. This is also a very high burden. And each prong of this two-part test provides ample opportunity for the trial judge, and later the appellate court if you decide to appeal the trial judge's ruling, to reject your argument that your trial lawyer was ineffective, and to reject your request for a new trial.

Trial lawyers, of course, hate ineffective assistance of counsel claims. Often these claims are nothing more than sour grapes from defendants who don't like the outcomes in their cases, and are looking to blame anyone they can. Further, the allegations against the trial lawyers are often incredibly nitpicky claims, crafted by appellate lawyers who sometimes have never experienced the stress of a jury trial. Despite this, and with the benefit of hindsight, appellate lawyers will (and must) vigorously advocate for the client and comb the transcript for anything the trial lawyer may have done wrong that could serve as the basis for a new trial.

■ ■ ■

Many criminal trial lawyers, including state public defenders, are incredibly dedicated, hardworking, bright, and resourceful, despite the nearly impossible demands and workload placed upon them by the criminal justice system.[10] And in most cases, these lawyers do more than a constitutionally effective job. But sometimes, for any number of reasons—including a complete lack of knowledge and training—defense lawyers will screw up at trial and not even come close to rendering effective assistance to their clients. In these cases, the problem, once again, is that this constitutional right to the effective assistance of counsel is so soft and malleable that it can be bent any which way the prosecutor and judge choose. Remember that their goal is to anoint your trial lawyer's performance as constitutionally effective, if not brilliant, no matter how ineffective it may actually have been. If they can accomplish that, then your conviction will be preserved, and the prosecutor won't have to retry the case and actually risk losing it.

Let's demonstrate how this works by placing you square in the middle of a set of facts adapted from a published case.[11] You are charged with a serious felony: robbery by use of force. Your accuser, a convicted criminal many times over, says that you simply walked up to him, out of the blue, and robbed him of his money. This is the only evidence against you, and the accuser is the state's only substantive witness at trial. You testify at trial in your own defense, but you are convicted nonetheless. The jury believed him instead of you, and now you're serving a fifteen-year prison sentence.

You decide to appeal your conviction and, after analyzing the case, your state-appointed appellate lawyer says that your trial lawyer performed miserably; that is, he was definitely ineffective, and the trial judge might award you a new trial. You agree with the strategy to go after your trial lawyer, and your appellate lawyer subpoenas him as a witness at the postconviction motion hearing. The testimony at that hearing, designed to show that your trial lawyer was ineffective, goes something like this:

Appellate Lawyer: Mr. Trial Lawyer, the accuser in this case testified at a preliminary hearing *before* trial, where he told quite a different story from the one he told *at* trial. But you never got the transcript from that earlier hearing, and you were therefore unable to impeach him at trial and expose him as a liar, correct?

Trial Lawyer: You are correct. I didn't think to order the transcript of his earlier testimony. I just figured he would tell the same story at trial.

Appellate Lawyer: Mr. Trial Lawyer, the prosecutor in this case told the jury that your client exercised his right to remain silent and refused to talk to police, thereby implying to the jury that your client was guilty. The prosecutor did this in his opening statement, during trial, and in closing argument. Yet you did not object to this improper tactic, did you?

Trial Lawyer: No, I didn't. I was not familiar with the law on a defendant's pre-*Miranda* right to remain silent. I thought it was admissible evidence, but it really wasn't, at least not under the facts of our case. That's my mistake.

Appellate Lawyer: Mr. Trial Lawyer, you knew about an eyewitness to this alleged robbery who would have confirmed your client's version of the events, but you did not call that person as a witness, or even talk to that person before trial, did you?

Trial Lawyer: No, I didn't. I wanted to keep it simple at trial. The fewer witnesses the better.

Appellate Lawyer: Mr. Trial Lawyer, you had a state-funded private investigator at your disposal, but you failed to conduct any investigation whatsoever, and you failed to subpoena the eyewitnesses to the alleged crime, isn't that true?

Trial Lawyer: That's true. I didn't think the jury would convict based on the accuser's word alone, so my strategy, again, was to keep it simple.

Appellate Lawyer: Mr. Trial Lawyer, the prosecutor in this case made improper comments in his closing argument, including saying that the role of a defense lawyer was *not* to "do justice," but simply "to get the guilty guys off." Yet you did not object to this, did you?

Trial Lawyer: No, I didn't. I didn't realize that was improper argument. Again, that was my mistake.

At this point you're thinking that you wish you'd had this new appellate lawyer, instead of your old trial lawyer, a lot sooner. You're also thinking that this hearing is going pretty well. Your trial lawyer screwed up all over the place. He just admitted that he literally did no investigation whatsoever, didn't even know the law regarding key legal issues, and didn't subpoena any witnesses that could have helped your case.

Your enthusiasm would indeed be justified. In fact, the court ruled that the trial lawyer's performance failed to live up to the constitutionally mandated standard; that is, the court branded the trial lawyer as ineffective. But—and yes, there is a *but* here—don't forget the second half of the two-pronged test for whether you received ineffective assistance of counsel. Not only do you have to prove that your trial lawyer screwed up, but you also have to prove that it was his screwup, and not something else, such as your guilt, that caused you to lose your trial. That should be pretty easy in this case, you're thinking. After all, the state didn't have any evidence, other than the accusation. And the accuser was even a convicted criminal several times over. So had your trial lawyer done his job, you probably would have won your case.

Unfortunately for you, however, the right to the effective assistance of counsel is a soft law, just like your other constitutional rights. The trial judge, then the appellate court, and then the state supreme court after that decided that although your trial lawyer screwed up multiple times, you simply didn't carry your burden to prove that the screwups, rather than something else, led to your conviction. That is, you failed the second prong of the test, and you lose. No new trial for you.

The problem with this legal standard—the two-pronged test for proving ineffective assistance of counsel and getting a new trial—is that it is nearly *impossible* to prove that the screwup, and not something else, led to your conviction. In fact, one of the concurring justices in the case on which our hypothetical example is based wrote:

> Because the defendant has failed to show that a reasonable probability exists that the result of the proceeding would have been different, I join the majority opinion [to uphold the conviction]. That does not mean that I agree that defendant has not been prejudiced here; he has. His attorney admitted that he did no independent investigation. Potential witnesses have thus been forever lost. Absent any additional witnesses, defendant has consequently failed to meet his requisite burden of showing the level of prejudice needed to overturn the conviction. I write separately because this case illustrates the difficulties this court has in determining *whether the defendant can ever* show the requisite amount of prejudice necessary to overturn a conviction when a defense attorney fails to investigate the case, and potential evidence favorable to the defense is forever lost. . . . *The result in this case, while legally correct, should disturb us all.* [12]

Despite this warning, few people were actually disturbed. Rather, the two-pronged test is exactly the way the legal system wants it. If the test were a reasonable one, instead of an impossible one, then defendants would be getting new trials, and their trial lawyers would be required to know the applicable law, investigate cases, and possibly even call witnesses. And if enough cases had to be retried over and over again, then there might even be a clamoring to change legal education or legal licensing requirements so that lawyers were actually trained to practice law. This would be real reform. And to set the wheels of reform into motion, the state supreme court should have issued an opinion something like this:

> The defendant has brought a motion for a new trial on the basis that his trial counsel was ineffective. The state's case consisted merely of an allegation, with no supporting evidence. The trial lawyer, by his own admission, failed to investigate the case before trial. He also failed to talk to or subpoena *any* eyewitnesses. He even failed to call the one witness who would have supported the defendant's story in this very weak, "he-said-he-said" criminal case. Then, during trial, counsel made multiple errors during the opening statements, during the presentation of evidence, and again in closing arguments—essentially, in every phase of the case. He even admitted, to his credit, that he was uninformed about the law. He's batting zero here. Can we really have any confidence that justice was done in this case? Of course we cannot. Let's give the defendant a new trial with a new trial attorney. Let's get it right, or at least close to right, the second time. The conviction must be reversed and the defendant is entitled to a new trial. [13]

But that's not what the state supreme court—or at least the majority of the state supreme court—decided. Instead, they looked for any excuse, no matter how disingenuous or intellectually weak, to preserve the defendant's conviction, and they were awfully creative in doing so. Although the trial lawyer fell asleep on the job (only figuratively, in this case) and committed multiple errors, the appellate court, and later the state supreme court, easily got around this problem.

First, the state supreme court merely said that the *number* of defense counsel's errors, relative to the number of *pages* in the trial transcript, constituted too low a numerical ratio to conclude that the errors led to the conviction. This nonsensical reasoning, of course, completely ignores the *impact* of the errors, regardless of whether the defense lawyer screwed up one time or one hundred times. And second, the state supreme court looked at the errors in isolation, rather than as a whole, and decided that, individually, none of them warranted a new trial. Then, it was only a small leap from there to decide that, even cumulatively, the errors didn't warrant a new trial.

Essentially, judges at all levels will do and say whatever is necessary, often with straight faces, in order to preserve defendants' convictions. In fairness, one justice in the above case—Justice Louis Butler, who was discussed in the introduction of this book—was highly critical of the legal standard itself. And another justice—Chief Justice Shirley Abrahamson—was not only critical of the legal standard, but even went a step further and dissented, meaning that she voted to overturn the defendant's conviction. But all of that is of little consolation to you if you're the defendant in the case, who must now serve a long prison sentence because your trial lawyer completely dropped the ball.

But wait—there may be some comforting news for you, after all. Some defendants have it much worse than you did. Some defendants have trial lawyers who not only did a bad job, but who *literally* fell asleep during trial. Surely, that would *have* to be ineffective assistance of counsel, right? Surely, those defendants were granted new trials, weren't they? Don't bet on it. Courts have bent over so far backward to preserve convictions, it's no small wonder their metaphorical backs haven't broken. In at least one case of a sleeping defense attorney—and, more specifically, a defense attorney who slept during the prosecutor's cross-examination *of his own client*—the courts refused to grant a new trial. The reason? Well, even though the prosecutor scored a lot of points for the government's case during the defense lawyer's nap time, the defendant "fail[ed] to show that there is a reasonable probability his counsel could have prevented either of these prejudicial events from occurring *had he been awake*—much less that it would have affected the outcome of the trial."[14]

For a prosecutor to argue, and for a court to rule, that a defense lawyer can sleep during the prosecutor's cross-examination of his own client, yet still be constitutionally *effective* completely degrades, and nearly abolishes, the right to the effective assistance of counsel.[15]

■ ■ ■

So there you have it. Our constitutional rights at first appear serious, strong, and even majestic—at least on paper. But in reality, it's quite a different story. The obvious question is, what can we do about this current state of affairs? That is the topic of the next, and final, chapter.

NOTES

1. "In all criminal prosecutions, the accused shall enjoy the right . . . to have the assistance of counsel for his defense." United States Constitution, Sixth Amendment, at www.law.cornell.edu/constitution/sixth_amendment (accessed December 3, 2011).
2. *Strickland v. Washington*, 466 U.S. 688 (1984).
3. Ellie Mystal, "Clients Won't Pay for What Law Schools Churn Out," October 17, 2011, at abovethelaw.com/2011/10/clients-wont-pay-for-what-law-schools-churn-out/ (accessed December 3, 2011).
4. Nate Oman, "'Doing What We Do Best' or 'Why Law Professors Should Feel Less Guilt,'" April 7, 2008, at madisonian.net/2008/04/07/doing-what-we-do-best-or-why-law-professors-should-feel-less-guilt/ (accessed December 3, 2011).
5. David Hricik and Victoria S. Salzmann, "Why There Should Be Fewer Articles Like This One: Law Professors Should Write More for Legal Decision-Makers and Less for Themselves," 38 *Suffolk University Law Review* 761 (2005), at www.law.suffolk.edu/highlights/stuorgs/lawreview/documents/HricikSalzmann.pdf (accessed December 3, 2011).
6. David Lat, "Bring Back Apprenticeships," *New York Times*, July 25, 2011, at www.nytimes.com/roomfordebate/2011/07/21/the-case-against-law-school/bring-back-apprenticeships-in-legal-education (accessed December 3, 2011).
7. *Strickland v. Washington*, 466 U.S. 688 (1984).
8. See Jonathan H. Adler, "How Long a Nap Is Ineffective Assistance of Counsel?" July 30, 2011, at volokh.com/2011/07/30/how-long-a-nap-is-ineffective-assistance-of-counsel/ (accessed December 3, 2011); and "Habeas—Ineffective Assistance–Sleeping Counsel," On Point by the Wisconsin State Public Defender, August 25, 2011, at www.wisconsinappeals.net/?p=6171 (accessed December 4, 2011).
9. *State v. Mayo*, 2007 WI 78.
10. Erik Eckholm, "Citing Workload, Public Lawyers Reject New Cases," *New York Times*, November 8, 2008, at www.nytimes.com/2008/11/09/us/09defender.html?pagewanted=all (accessed December 4, 2011).
11. The hypothetical example in this chapter is loosely based on *State v. Mayo*.
12. Ibid. (concurring opinion).
13. This hypothetical court ruling is loosely based on the dissenting opinion, *State v. Mayo*.
14. *Muniz v. Smith*, No. 09-2324 (6th Cir. 2011; emphasis added).
15. It appears, however, that if a defense lawyer is "repeatedly unconscious through [substantial] portions of the defendant's capital murder trial," then the defendant might get a new trial. *Burdine v. Johnson*, 262 F.3d 336 (5th Cir. 2001).

Chapter Fifteen

Moving Forward

It is fitting that I begin writing this final chapter on July 4. As we begin our annual celebration of our independence from the British Crown, many of us are blissfully unaware of the tremendous reach that our own government agents have into our lives. In fact, the power given to police, prosecutors, and judges would probably shock the framers of the Constitution if they were alive to witness it.[1] Government has grown well beyond anything they could possibly have envisioned, and its expansiveness has, without question, negatively impacted our individual constitutional rights.

Hopefully, in the first three chapters of this book, I convinced you of the incredible importance of these rights and illustrated why, in order to be effective for anyone, they must be applied equally to everyone. Then, in the remaining chapters, I hope I've effectively demonstrated how our government agents go about sidestepping or flat-out destroying these rights. If I have done these things persuasively, then we have taken the first important step. But the critical question remains: How do we actually fix the problem? How do we restore the backbone to our constitutional rights? Perhaps more to the point, how do we take back our rights from the police, prosecutors, and judges who have trivialized them beyond belief and treat them, in many cases, as a minor obstacle in their path to obtaining criminal convictions?

It is important to understand where we should *not* look for answers. Most obviously, as this book has demonstrated, we should *not* look to the courts or even to the United States Supreme Court.

When I was in law school, a professor asked us this question: "How are the United States Supreme Court's decisions enforced?" This wasn't a question that I had thought about up to that point, and I definitely wasn't able to answer it on the spot. And, although the question did, admittedly, catch enough of my attention that I can still remember it today, I really wasn't particularly interested in the answer. In fact, I don't even remember what the answer was, assuming that the professor even gave one. (Law school classes are notorious for purposely leaving matters unresolved.) All I knew—or thought I knew—was that Supreme Court decisions *were* enforced, and I just wasn't terribly interested in learning *how* that was done.

Today, however, I realize that the problem lies in the question itself. By asking *how* something is done—here, "how are the United States Supreme Court's decisions enforced?"—the questioner craftily sneaks in the assumption that the thing in question *is* being done. But isn't this is a perfectly reasonable assumption for Supreme Court decisions? After all, we live in a nation that is built on the rule of law. Of course the decisions of our highest court are being enforced, even if the mechanism for doing so is somewhat mysterious. This simply must be true.

But in reality, we have seen that the Supreme Court's decisions are *not* being enforced. And in many cases, this is because they are far too vague to be enforced. For example, even though our Supreme Court has admitted that "judges, like other government officers, could not always be trusted to safe-guard the rights of the people,"[2] the Court still refuses to write a confrontation-clause decision that imposes any level of structure or constraint on these government officers. Instead, the Court writes vague, ultraflexible, and overly wordy decisions. (The Court has the uncanny ability to write dozens of pages while communicating nothing of substance.) These decisions, in turn, give police, prosecutors, and judges more than enough rope to hang any defendant they wish, for any reason. We've seen multiple examples of this so far. In fact, you can turn to any chapter in this book to learn, in step-by-step detail, precisely how they are violating numerous different rights, all the while operating under the wandering (or nonexistent) eye of the Supreme Court.

So, if our flaccid Supreme Court refuses to take our constitutional rights seriously, what can we do? The answer is, in one sense, very simple. We need to turn the criminal justice system and our individual rights into issues for serious political debate. We need to elevate them above the typical topics of political contention like gay marriage, flag burning, abortion, or even the flat tax. In fact, given the billions of dollars we pour into our various wars on crime every year—including the cost of housing 25 percent of the *world's* prisoners—it would be wise to demand that our legislative candidates go beyond mere sound bites such as "tough on crime." We must demand that they actually explain the substance of their views—which, of course, would require them to actually *have* views—on the criminal justice system. Once we elevate these topics to this level of discourse, we then need to elect our legislators accordingly.

More specifically, we need legislators who are willing to rein in the power of the police, prosecutors, and judges. We need legislators who will be bold enough to do two things: first, decriminalize some behavior; and second, simplify our system of criminal procedure by implementing some basic, firm, and clear rules. This is not pie-in-the-sky thinking, especially in today's state of governmental fiscal crisis. That is, these two goals—decriminalization and procedural simplification—would not only strengthen our individual rights, but would also save billions of dollars for our federal and state governments. And if the issues are framed in such a way that they are tied to taxpayer pocketbooks, the issues will suddenly become important.

While this book is not the place to draft a comprehensive political platform, some brief examples are in order. The first of the two reforms—decriminalization—involves removing crimes from the criminal code and reducing penalties. This would, of course, constrain the power of the police who arrest us, the prosecutors who prosecute us, and the judges who sentence us. For example, the crime of disorderly conduct should be decriminalized. Disorderly conduct is a relatively minor crime, but by far the most common crime for which young adults are arrested, convicted, and sentenced.[3] These cases cost the taxpayers a great deal of our money by consuming the time and resources of the entire criminal justice system, including the department of corrections and the prison system. Instead, disorderly conduct could be handled quite easily by the revenue-*generating* means of a local ordinance ticket. And if a person's disorderly conduct is so serious as to be dangerous, then it will already be charged as criminal battery, criminal reckless endangerment of safety, or any one of dozens of other crimes. Therefore, no one would be harmed, and we citizens would benefit financially, if the disorderly-conduct criminal statute were simply to disappear.

Similarly, we could limit the reach that police, prosecutors, and judges have into our lives by decriminalizing other things, such as first-time marijuana possession for personal use, operating a motor vehicle with a suspended or revoked license, consensual sex between teenagers and young adults, and dozens of other acts that don't harm anyone or, even if they do, still shouldn't be criminalized. It is these types of crimes, and not the relatively small number of armed robberies or murders, that ensnare so many people in the system and clog up our courts. In fact, in the federal courts, the impact of overcriminalization is even being felt by big businesses. Corporations can no longer have their contract disputes and intellectual-property litigation resolved because they're being crowded-out by federal criminal cases. The *Wall Street Journal* reports that "the proliferation of more-obscure federal criminal laws" has created a logjam and "threatens the functioning of the nation's judicial system."[4]

Further, for things that should be, and are, criminalized, the penalty schemes are often unbelievably draconian and should be scaled back. The most extreme example, of course, is California's fiscal disaster known as "three strikes and you're in." This scheme has incarcerated huge numbers of people for decades or even life for crimes as minor as misdemeanor retail theft.[5] California's slow-moving train wreck of a criminal justice system is an entire book in itself. And the Golden State isn't alone; in other states, even relatively benign acts often fall within felony criminal statues that carry decades of incarceration. However, the point for our purposes is that we want legislators who will draft reasonable penalty schemes that will constrain judicial discretion.

But decriminalization is only one possible legislative reform. The second of these reforms is procedural simplification. Procedurally, the criminal justice system is a vague, mushy set of so-called rules that can be molded to achieve any outcome desired by those in power. These rules give far too much discretion and power to government agents, and offer virtually no protection of our individual rights.

Here is an example of procedural simplification that would create consistency and predictability, and would also help unclog our court system. Suppose that the parties to a criminal case agree as follows: the prosecutor will dismiss count 1 of a criminal complaint; the defendant will plead to count 2 of that complaint; and the prosecutor will recommend probation on that count. Then, after the agreement is reached, the defendant has to enter his plea, where he puts himself at the mercy of the trial judge who is *not* bound by the plea agreement. The judge must dismiss count 1, as agreed, and the parties will make their probation recommendation. However, the judge is not bound by recommendations; instead, he can impose whatever sentence he wishes.

At the sentencing hearing, instead of imposing the joint recommendation, the judge suddenly decides that probation is *not* in the best interest of the community. He instead exercises his judicial discretion and sentences the defendant to a decade in prison. Postconviction motions and appeals follow, and the issues include whether the prosecutor breached the plea agreement by not wholeheartedly recommending probation, whether the judge abused his discretion or considered impermissible factors when sentencing the defendant, whether the defense lawyer was ineffective for any number of reasons, and whether the defendant can now withdraw his guilty plea and go to trial instead. What was intended to quickly and easily resolve the case has exploded into a litigious nightmare for years to come. Thousands of cases like this will consume the time and resources of the entire court system—all at taxpayer expense.

For states that have a plea bargaining system like this, the solution is simple. Just as legislatures pass laws constraining, for example, a landlord's power in rental agreements, so too can the legislatures pass laws constraining a judge's power in plea agreements. And they can do it simply by requiring judges to use their discretion *before* the defendant enters a plea and puts him- or herself at the judge's mercy. Here's how it would work: If the prosecutor and the defendant reach a plea agreement, which they do in more than 90 percent of cases, they would be required to put the agreement in writing and submit it to the judge for approval. Then, the judge can either approve it, in which case he must allow the parties to enforce the terms of their bargain, including the agreed-upon sentence; or he can reject it because it is not in the best interest of the community, in which case the parties can start negotiations from scratch, or go to trial instead. (And if the judge is undecided, he can hold a hearing and ask the parties all the questions he wants before deciding whether to accept the plea agreement.)

With the threat of multiday or multiweek trials hanging over their heads, rather than the more convenient (and fun) option of slamming helpless defendants with prison *after* they've entered into plea bargains for probation, judges would magically start deciding that these proposed plea agreements *were* in the best interest of the community. (It's funny how the exercise of judicial discretion can lead to dramatically different results when the judge's time is at stake.) This type of law would still allow judges to protect the interests of the community—something the prosecutor is already doing anyway—by rejecting plea bargains, but it would take away their power to impose arbitrary and draconian punishment. How? By requiring them to exercise their judicial discretion *before* a defendant enters a plea.

And from a financial standpoint, immeasurable resources would be saved because there would be nothing to litigate after the plea deal was accepted. That is, defendants would have nothing to appeal once they get the precise terms, including the recommended sentence, for which they bargained. And considering that more than 90 percent of cases resolve by plea bargain, and that most litigation involves plea bargains in some way, the court system would instantly flow much more freely, and would be far more fair and predictable. And this is just one example. The possibilities for procedural simplification are endless, and start from the time the charges are filed and extend through the sentencing hearing.

But this only covers the election of our legislators, so we're just getting started. When we citizens elect our district attorneys, we need to elect those who are rational, thoughtful, and not overly punitive. For example, the voters in one Wisconsin county elected a prosecutor who made national headlines by threatening to criminally charge schoolteachers for teaching sex education. And he threatened this even though the sex-education program they were teaching had already been approved by the state legislature, and parents even had the option of taking their children out of the program.[6] The district attorney's reasoning? The teachers were contributing to the delinquency of minors because when minors have consensual sex it could constitute felony sexual assault of a child, depending on their ages. Of course, this district attorney's stance was only one step removed from charging the teachers with the far more serious crime of aiding and abetting a felony sexual assault of a child. And if you don't think that is possible, you should know that prosecutors have charged defendants with, and convicted defendants of, aiding and abetting sexual assault for doing far *less* than teaching sex education.[7] This is the type of prosecutorial nonsense that we citizens should not tolerate.

And when we citizens elect our trial judges, we need to elect judges who will exercise some reasonableness, practicality, and restraint. After all, no matter how good of a job the legislature does in drafting laws and procedures, there will always be some need for judicial discretion. We need to elect judges who, instead of using buzzwords and phrases like "tough on crime," talk about being reasonable on crime and, on the other hand, also talk about protecting individual constitutional rights. We need to elect judges who recognize the difference between victimless crimes and true victims of crime, and who understand that their role is to serve the citizenry, and not the police or prosecutor. Today, many trial judges don't view themselves as public servants, but rather as an arm of the prosecutor's office. As we saw in chapter 9, one judge even proudly told the jury, before a defendant's trial, that he was part of law enforcement. And judges do this because we allow them to get away with it.

■ ■ ■

As I indicated at the beginning of this chapter, however, only in *one sense* is the solution very simple. In another sense, and as a practical matter, strengthening our constitutional rights will not happen quickly or easily. We citizens simply are not likely to elevate our constitutional rights to be on par with issues such as abortion or gay marriage. And this is somewhat paradoxical. Although gay marriage, for example, doesn't negatively impact any of us, many of us still go to great lengths and much effort to oppose it. Conversely, the violation of the constitutional rights discussed in this book could negatively affect every one of us; yet relatively few of us are even remotely interested in the subject.

This paradox may well be due to several common misconceptions—misconceptions that this book has attempted to dispel—including the belief that only morally bad people are accused of, prosecuted for, and convicted of crimes. This belief, in fact, is on full display in criminal jury trials. During the jury-selection process, many potential jurors candidly state that, because the defendant sits before them at the defense table, he or she *must* be guilty of a crime. They are assuming, of course, that the criminal justice system always works, and that police and prosecutors only go after the bad guys.

On one hand, I am incredibly grateful when potential jurors share this belief before a trial; without their honesty, it would be impossible to assemble a fair and impartial jury. (Although I wonder how many other jurors hold this same view but are too timid to express it.) But on the other hand, I am amazed by the thought process behind the presumption of guilt, especially in light of public examples to the contrary. No doubt all of us have heard of at least one false-accusation case—for example, the Duke lacrosse scandal—or one wrongful conviction—for example, the Central Park jogger case. Yet unlike when we hear about other disastrous events—for example, plane crashes or terrorist attacks—we do not fear that false accusations or wrongful convictions could happen to us. In fact, our presumption of guilt seems to apply only to *other people*. That is, when others are being prosecuted for crimes, they are no doubt guilty; but if I were to be prosecuted, not only would I be innocent (that goes without saying), but I would also demand to feast at the entire smorgasbord of constitutional rights.

The solution to this misconception is, once again, education—education about our constitutional rights, about what can happen to us if those rights are not strong, and about what *really* happens to ordinary people on a daily basis in the world of criminal justice. I hope that I have advanced that type of education with this book.

"Where we go from there is a choice I leave to you."[8]

NOTES

1. In *Crawford v. Washington*, 541 U.S. 36 (2004), for example, the Court stated that "[t]he Framers would be astounded to learn that *ex parte* testimony could be admitted against a criminal defendant because it was elicited by 'neutral' government officers." The police, of course, are anything but neutral, yet this assumption pervades not only our popular culture but also many courts.

2. *Crawford v. Washington.*

3. Eileen Hirsch, Ginger Murray, and Wendy Henderson, "Raising the Age: Return Seventeen-Year-Olds to Juvenile Court," figure 1, *Wisconsin Lawyer*, June 2007, at www.wisbar.org/AM/Template.cfm?Section=Wisconsin_Lawyer&Template=/CM/ContentDisplay.cfm&CONTENTID=65278#fl (accessed December 5, 2011).

4. Gary Fields and John Emshwiller, "Criminal Case Glut Impedes Civil Suits," *Wall Street Journal*, November 10, 2011, at http://online.wsj.com/article/SB10001424052970204505304577001771159867642.html?mod=ITP_pageone_0 (accessed December 5, 2011).

5. Laura Gottesdiener, "California Prison Legislation Is among the Most Punitive in the Nation," *Huffington Post*, May 27, 2011, at http://www.huffingtonpost.com/2011/05/27/california-prison-legislation_n_868326.html (accessed December 5, 2011).

6. Ed Brayton, "Wingnut Prosecutor Threatens Teachers," Dispatches from the Creation Wars, April 8, 2010, at scienceblogs.com/dispatches/2010/04/wingnut_prosecutor_threatens_t.php (accessed December 5, 2011).

7. Michael D. Cicchini, "Guilt by Association," the Legal Watchdog, January 22, 2011, at thelegalwatchdog.blogspot.com/2011/01/guilt-by-association.html (accessed December 5, 2011).

8. *The Matrix*, dir. Andy and Lana Wachowski, perf. Keanu Reeves as Neo, DVD, Warner Bros., 1999.

Further Reading

Alschuler, Albert W. "Studying the Exclusionary Rule: An Empirical Classic." 75 *University of Chicago Law Review* 1365 (2008).

Baugh, Whitney. "Why the Sky Didn't Fall: Using Judicial Creativity to Circumvent *Crawford v. Washington*." 38 *Loyola Los Angeles Law Review* 1835 (2005).

Chin, Gabriel J., and Scott C. Wells. "The 'Blue Wall of Silence' as Evidence of Bias and Motive to Lie: A New Approach to Police Perjury." 59 *University of Pittsburgh Law Review* 233 (1998).

Chojnacki, Danielle E., Michael D. Cicchini, and Lawrence T. White. "An Empirical Basis for the Admission of Expert Testimony on False Confessions." 40 *Arizona State Law Journal* 1 (2008).

Cicchini, Michael D. "Broken Government Promises: A Contract-Based Approach to Enforcing Plea Bargains." 38 *New Mexico Law Review* 159 (2008).

Cicchini, Michael D. "Dead Again: The Latest Demise of the Confrontation Clause." 80 *Fordham Law Review* 1301 (2011).

Cicchini, Michael D. "An Economics Perspective on the Exclusionary Rule and Deterrence." 75 *Missouri Law Review* 459 (2010).

Cicchini, Michael D. "Judicial (In)Discretion: How Courts Circumvent the Confrontation Clause under *Crawford* and *Davis*." 75 *Tennessee Law Review* 753 (2009).

Cicchini, Michael D. "Prosecutorial Misconduct at Trial: A New Perspective Rooted in Confrontation Clause Jurisprudence." 37 *Seton Hall Law Review* 335 (2007).

Cicchini, Michael D., and Joseph Easton. "Reforming the Law on Show-Up Identifications." 100 *Journal of Criminal Law and Criminology* 381 (2010).

Cicchini, Michael D., and Vincent Rust. "Confrontation after *Crawford v. Washington*: Defining Testimonial." 10 *Lewis and Clark Law Review* 531 (2006).

Cook, Julian A. III. "All Aboard! The Supreme Court, Guilty Pleas, and the Railroading of Criminal Defendants." 75 *University of Colorado Law Review* 863 (2004).

Davies, Sharon L. "The Penalty of Exclusion: A Price or Sanction?" 73 *Southern California Law Review* 1275 (2000).

Davis, Angela J. "The American Prosecutor: Independence, Power, and the Threat of Tyranny." 86 *Iowa Law Review* 393 (2001).

Duffy, Brian C. "Barring Foul Blows: An Argument for a Per Se Reversible-Error Rule for Prosecutors' Use of Religious Arguments in the Sentencing Phase of Capital Cases." 50 *Vanderbilt Law Review* 1335 (1997).

Gershman, Bennett L. "The New Prosecutors." 53 *University of Pittsburgh Law Review* 393 (1992).

Halliburton, Christian. "Leveling the Playing Field: A New Theory of Exclusion for a Post–PATRIOT Act America." 70 *Missouri Law Review* 519 (2005).

Hoeffel, Janet C. "Prosecutorial Discretion at the Core: The Good Prosecutor Meets Brady." 109 *Penn State Law Review* 1133 (2005).

Jaros, David. "The Lessons of *People v. Moscat*: Confronting Judicial Bias in Domestic Violence Cases Interpreting *Crawford v. Washington*." 42 *American Criminal Law Review* 995 (2005).

Kaiser, David A. "*United States v. Coon*: The End of Detrimental Reliance for Plea Agreements?" 52 *Hastings Law Journal* 579 (2001).

Kaplan, Daniel F. "Where Promises End: Prosecutorial Adherence to Sentence Recommendation Commitments in Plea Bargains." 52 *University of Chicago Law Review* 751 (1985).

Kirst, Roger W. "Does *Crawford* Provide a Stable Foundation for Confrontation Doctrine?" 71 *Brooklyn Law Review* 35 (2005).

Latcovich, Simon, ed. *Thirty-Fifth Annual Review of Criminal Procedure*. Georgetown Law Journal, 2006.

Monico, Michael, and Barry Spevack. *Federal Criminal Practice: A Seventh Circuit Handbook*. Mathew Bender, 2005.

Oaks, Daniel H. "Studying the Exclusionary Rule in Search and Seizure." 37 *University of Chicago Law Review* 665 (1969).

Rosenthal, Kenneth. "Prosecutor Misconduct, Convictions, and Double Jeopardy: Case Studies in an Emerging Jurisprudence." 71 *Temple Law Review* 887 (1998).

Ross, Josephine. "After *Crawford* Double-Speak: 'Testimony' Does Not Mean Testimony and 'Witness' Does Not Mean Witness." 97 *Journal of Criminal Law and Criminology* 147 (2006).

Scott, Robert E., and William J. Stuntz. "Plea Bargaining as Contract." 101 *Yale Law Journal* 1909 (1992).

Spiegelman, Paul J. "Prosecutorial Misconduct in Closing Argument: The Role of Intent in Appellate Review." 1 *Journal of Appellate Practice and Process* 115 (1999).

Stevens, Elizabeth, J. "Deputy-Doctors: The Medical Treatment Exception after *Davis v. Washington*." 43 *California Western Law Review* 451 (2007).

Westen, Peter, and David Westin. "A Constitutional Law of Remedies for Broken Plea Bargains." 66 *California Law Review* 471 (1978).

White, Welsh. "Curbing Prosecutorial Misconduct in Capital Cases: Imposing Prohibitions on Improper Penalty Trial Arguments." 39 *American Criminal Law Review* 1147 (2002).

Wiseman, Christine, Nicholas Chiarkas, and Daniel D. Blinka. *Wisconsin Practice: Criminal Practice and Procedure*. St. Paul, MN: West, 1996.

Yaroshefsky, Ellen. "Zealous Advocacy in a Time of Uncertainty: Understanding Lawyers' Ethics; Wrongful Convictions—It Is Time to Take Prosecution Discipline Seriously." 8 *D.C. Law Review* 275 (2004).

Index

About the Author

Michael D. Cicchini is a criminal defense lawyer in Kenosha, Wisconsin. Based on his numerous trial wins in felony cases, he has been named among the "Top 100 Trial Lawyers" in Wisconsin by the National Trial Lawyers, and among the "Top Young Lawyers" in Wisconsin by Super Lawyers and *Milwaukee* magazine.

Cicchini is a coauthor of *But They Didn't Read Me My Rights! Myths, Oddities, and Lies about Our Legal System*, and the author of numerous articles on criminal and constitutional law, including "Dead Again: The Latest Demise of the Confrontation Clause." He also founded the Legal Watchdog blog, where he writes on legal topics and, occasionally, goes well outside of his range to speculate on college sports, politics, and even physics.

Cicchini earned his JD, *summa cum laude*, from Marquette University Law School, and also holds an MBA degree and a CPA certificate. More information, including the full text of his articles and a link to the Legal Watchdog, can be found at www.CicchiniLaw.com.